SELL
YOUR OWN
HOME!

SELL
YOUR OWN
HOME!

Up-To-Date
Money-Saving Strategies
That Work

Warren Boroson

Knight-Ridder Press

Tucson, AZ

Published by Knight-Ridder Press
A division of HPBooks, Inc.
P.O. Box 5367
Tucson, AZ 85703

Printed in U.S.A.
9 8 7 6 5 4 3 2
First printing

Library of Congress Cataloging-in-Publication Data

Boroson, Warren
Sell your own home!

  Includes index.
  1. House selling. I. Title.
HD1379.B645   1987   333.3'8   87-4020
ISBN 0-89586-556-4 (pb)
ISBN 0-89586-571-8 (cl)

Contents

HOW TO EARN $100 AN HOUR

Selling your house—or condominium, cooperative apartment, houseboat, whatever—without the help of
a real-estate agent is rarely a lead-pipe
cinch. But it's not so difficult as
neurosurgery, or trying to calculate
which life-insurance policy is cheap-
est. Indeed, the first lesson for any
do-it-yourselfer to learn is:

1. **Many homeowners try to sell their
   houses themselves, and many are
   successful.**

Homeowners sell their residences
to reputable people who have ample

1

means, they don't spend an inordinate amount of time on the whole business, and they wind up with a welcome boost to their self-esteem and a healthy addition to their net worth.

For evidence that do-it-yourselfers aren't eccentrics, Don Quixotes tilting at windmills, scan the real-estate advertisements in your local newspaper. Search for ads with the telltale words For Sale by Owner, or Principals Only. Sometimes the only clue is a phone number without the name of a broker.

Or drive through your town looking for for-sale signs that provide only a phone number, no broker's name. (Alas, it's true: Owners selling their homes by themselves tend to put up the most primitive and ugly for-sale signs imaginable—instead of having a commercial artist create the sign, or buying a ready-made one in a hardware store.)

All the books and pamphlets on the subject are further evidence that selling your house yourself is fairly common. These do-it-yourself books, by the way, are distinguished by (a) their brevity and (b) the triteness of their advice (bake cookies before visitors come; clear out your closets).

No one knows exactly how many people go the do-it-yourself route—how many try, how many succeed. Estimates of the success rate range from one in five homeowners to one in eleven. There is a report that the National Association of Realtors actually sponsored a poll several years ago, in Florida, but suppressed the findings because they were so discouraging—to agents. A lot more homeowners apparently sold their houses without agents than the agents had suspected.

No doubt the number of sell-it-yourselfers varies by time and location. When mortgage rates are fairly low, when money is available, and when there's pent-up demand for housing, more owners try to bypass agents—as is certainly the case right now. Another indication that this is a seller's market: Discount brokers have sprouted up again. I've even seen an advertisement for an agency that will write you a For Sale by Owner ad! The area of the country also has a bearing on how many homeowners try to do it themselves. In some places, "fizzbos"—real-estate people's term for sell-it-yourselfers, from For Sale By Owner (FSBO)—flourish. In other areas they are rare, perhaps because it just isn't traditional, and homeowners may be a trifle ashamed of letting their neighbors know that they're trying to save a little money. Probably people in the richer areas, and the poorer ones, rely unthinkingly on agents: the rich because they can readily afford an agent's fee and don't want to bother saving a "little" extra, and the not-so-well-to-do because they don't know any better.

But whether the truth is that one in five homeowners or one in eleven homeowners tries and succeeds in selling his or her house, it means that many people *do* succeed.

A second lesson for the first-time fizzbo is:

2. **You can save a good deal of money by selling your house yourself.**

If you sell an $80,000 house through an agent, you'll pay a 6 or 7 percent commission—say, $5,000. Selling the house yourself might take you 4 months and 40 hours of work, including everything from writing and placing ads to showing buyers through your house. Subtract $500–$1,000 for advertising, and you wind up with $4,000 for 40 hours of work. That's $100 an hour.

Of course, you may want to share some of the agent's commission with a buyer, just to bring about a faster sale. So you might drop your offering price by one-third or one-half the commission. But with a lower price on your house, you might spend only $500 on advertising—or even less. Your hourly salary would now be $50–$70.

If you're already earning $100,000 or $200,000 a year, then your house may be worth considerably more than the $80,000 in our example—and it might still be tempting to join the ranks of the fizzbos. You might save a $12,000 commission when you sell a $200,000 house. The hourly rate for that work: $300.

The flaw with all these delicious calculations, of course, is that you may wind up spending $500 to $1,000 on ads, put in 40 hours of work, and wind up with . . . a house for sale. In which case, you've earned $00 an hour. Less, because of the money you've laid out.

But there's a benefit you may not have thought about. While you're selling your house yourself, all sorts of agents will besiege you to list with them. Some may even volunteer to sell your house at a reduced commission. If you're selling your house for $80,000 and an agent will accept a 5 percent commission, not 6 percent, you've saved $800 right there. Get an agent down to 4 percent, and you're at $1,600—significantly more than your out-of-pocket costs. So your efforts will not have been in vain. (By the way, both salespeople and the brokers they work for are agents. A Realtor is a broker who belongs to the National Association of Realtors.)

Besides, even if you eventually sign with a broker, you may still escape a commission. Instead of giving the brokerage firm an "exclusive agency," insist on an "exclusive right to sell" or an "open listing." These arrangements mean that if you yourself find a buyer, you can skip the commission. And the publicity campaign about your house you launched earlier may bring in a belated buyer. Someone you showed your house to two months ago may decide to purchase it directly from you—and that means your broker is decommissioned.

Of course, some homeowners feel that they should keep real-estate agents employed. In fact, their neighbors or their friends or even their relatives may be agents, constantly wheedling and pleading for a listing.

But if you want to be profligate, give your money to a deserving charity. And tell yourself that by becoming a fizzbo you'll be helping to make the American economy more efficient.

There are far too many real-estate agents around. (The National Association of Realtors has 700,000 members.) Their number is bloated by part-timers, by people who never really decided what they "wanted to be when they grew up" and drifted into real estate. The enormous commissions that agents receive help keep the field crowded. Just by selling a few houses occasionally, an agent can make a pretty decent living.

Fizzbos may have other reasons for selling their houses themselves. Perhaps they don't like real-estate agents and don't want to deal with them.

Still, the basic reason, the healthiest reason, to become a fizzbo is to save money. Think of it not as cash you'll blow on a Caribbean vacation. Think of it as money you can invest to finance your children's college educations, or to keep you comfortable after you've retired.

So, when your neighbor the real-estate agent knocks on your door and says, "I hear you're thinking of selling your house. You'll sign with my brokerage firm, won't you?" your answer might be, "I'd like to try selling it myself, because I really could use the extra money."

Why don't more people try to sell their houses themselves?

Perhaps they're lazy. Or, in their area, it's undignified to do something so mercenary as to sell your own residence. Or they may have a friend or neighbor who would be miffed if they didn't hand over the listing.

But the main reason seems to be that homeowners are intimidated. And that brings us to one more lesson:

3. Selling your residence yourself is not that difficult.

Real-estate agents want you to believe that it is. One agent, whom I shall call Mrs. Jones, advises her colleagues in a best-selling book, "In the last two decades of this century, the need for your services as a real-estate professional will continue to grow because financing and other aspects of real-estate knowledge will continue to become ever more complex. This means that owners attempting to sell by themselves will encounter greater difficulties every year. To solve them, they will turn ever more to highly trained full-time real-estate professionals."

Another scenario is that, as house prices keep going up and up, and so do agents' commissions, more and more homeowners will try to save a bundle by becoming fizzbos.

Mrs. Jones's strategy to "de-fizz fizzbos," as she calls it, is simple. She puts on a show of being helpful, meanwhile trying to persuade the owner that selling a residence alone is akin to surgically removing your own appendix with kitchen utensils.

For example, one day she'll send you a blank seller's

net sheet, which helps you figure out what profit you'll escape with. "Here's the form we use to figure your net walkaway dollars," she writes. "Please feel free to give me a call if you don't have the formulas to figure out any of these items." She advises fellow agents, "Be sure you don't say, 'If you don't know how to figure out any of these items,' which implies that they're stupid if they can't."

No, just imply that you need special formulas to figure out something that anyone with a sixth-grade education can figure out (see below).

Figuring Your Profit

Credits
Selling price _____
Taxes in escrow[*] _____
Prepaid taxes _____
Prepaid house insurance _____
Oil in tank buyer will pay for _____
_____(Other)
TOTAL _____

Debits
First mortgage balance _____
Second mortgage balance _____
Prepayment penalty _____
Lawyer's fee _____
Abstract _____
Title insurance (possibly) _____
Appraisal (possibly) _____
Commission (let's hope not) _____
_____(Other)
TOTAL _____

Subtract total credits from total debits to get your
Estimated Net Profit _____

[*]Extra money your mortgage holder may be keeping to pay the next installment of your real-estate taxes.

13

That's just the beginning of the siege. Mrs. Jones goes on to give the fizzbo reprints of magazine articles on "why it's so tough to sell your own home," along with literature like "Government Financing Plans That May Be Available to Finance the Purchase of Your Home." As she explains, "This will necessarily be complex."

She also tells fledgling agents the following:

Creative financing: "Throw some jargon around here, and mention that it's not possible to cover this complex subject fully in this brief discussion."

Items you'll need to complete your sale: "List such things as termite inspections, roof inspections, appraisals, assessor's parcel numbers, legal descriptions, building permits for any improvements, title insurance, etc." (No, you won't need all of these; those you *might* need are a snap to obtain.)

Show homeowners a "reprint of the most complicated magazine or newspaper article you've come across recently that discusses housing prices, interest rates, and the availability of mortgage funds."

Preliminary title report: "Select an intricate report from your office's files of completed home resale transactions so the fizzbo will gain some insight into the complications that arise here." And on and on.

Mrs. Jones, as it happens, is one of the more scrupulous agents. She relates the story of another agent who left a lovely potted plant on the doorstep of a fizzbo's home one Sunday morning. On top of the plant was an envelope. Inside was a newspaper clipping about another local fizzbo who had been kidnapped and robbed at gunpoint by someone pretending to be a buyer. A note from the agent said, "Be sure this doesn't happen to you."

The same dire consequence will probably follow if you let a bank decide the terms of your loan, or a plumber decide how to waterproof your basement. The loan you receive may have tricky provisions that will cost a lot more interest than you imagined (for example, the money you receive may be minus the first repayment, thus effectively raising the interest rate). The plumber may talk about a luxurious French drain system instead of proposing that you simply have your gutters fixed.

Likewise, if you trust a real-estate agent who tells you that selling a house is just too difficult for poor little you, you may wind up giving the agent an exclusive agency listing—and underpricing your house as well (see Chapter 4, p. 53).

But evidently real-estate agents and their allies have been successful in persuading many homeowners that they're not capable of selling their own homes.

Successful fizzbos *do* seem to have a background in real estate. Or they happen to be self-reliant, self-confident people to begin with. And because you are reading this book, I assume that you yourself aren't easily intimidated and you don't give up easily.

That's why you will probably be able to sell your house or condominium or cooperative or what-have-you by yourself, saving thousands of dollars.

With satisfaction Mrs. Jones reports that this unsavory specimen is now out of the real-estate business.

Besides, the practice of trying to "win by intimidation" has a long and inglorious history. Back in 1967 another agent/author counseled fellow agents to give fizzbos this list of questions—"*without* answers being included":

WHAT WOULD YOU DO, MR. HOME OWNER,
IF A PROSPECT ASKS YOU . . .

- ☐ for the CRV?
- ☐ the FHA evaluation?
- ☐ how much it takes to amortize $1,000 at 6 percent interest over a 25-year period?
- ☐ how much interest he would save if he financed the mortgage on a 20-year basis, at 6 percent, rather than for 25 years?
- ☐ how much principal will be paid on the first trust after 38 months?
- ☐ what he has to do when his second trust note (if there is one) becomes due and payable?

The CRV is a "certificate of reasonable value," required for loans guaranteed by the Veterans Administration. The other questions should be directed to a lender, not a seller. (A "trust note" is the term used in some states for a mortgage.)

I'm not picking on real-estate agents. Other people with something to sell may also try to intimidate and befuddle potential customers. For two reasons:

1. The customer may be induced to employ the seller.
   For example, you don't need a stockbroker or financial planner to help you choose a good mutual fund of stocks to buy. You can just visit a library, find a newsletter on mutual funds, and look for those that have outstanding track records and charge no commissions. But if you wind up with a stockbroker or financial planner, she will doubtless recommend a fund that will pay her a commission. Commissions can erode 8-1/2 percent of your investment.

Granted, selling your house yourself is more time consuming and arduous than choosing a mutual fund. But not by much.

2. The customer may allow the seller to make the key decisions.

Let's say you cannot decide whether you should buy whole-life insurance or term insurance. In the face of seemingly impenetrable complexity, you surrender and let an insurance agent choose for you. The agent, naturally, will sell you the policy that pays him the higher commission—namely, whole-life insurance.

IMPROVE BEFORE YOU MOVE?

2

It's surprising how many people hurry to remodel their homes just before they sell, hoping to make a quick and lavish profit. Says Arthur M. Watkins, author of *How to Avoid the Ten Biggest Home-Buying Traps,* "Spruce up your house before you sell, but in general don't spend big bucks trying to increase a house's resale value. It's too risky. If you do feel you should remodel before you sell, your best bet is a good kitchen—with the emphasis on 'good.'"

In terms of getting your money back, and perhaps more, *the best renovations solve inherent defects in your house:* new kitchens for old, an extra bathroom in a house that needs another (one and a half baths for every two bedrooms is the rule), a third bedroom in a house that has only two, a family room near the kitchen, new closets in a house with stingy storage space. Overall, your best bets are *new kitchens and bathrooms, extra living space, and a fireplace.*

What are the chances of your getting your money back? The National Association of the Remodeling Industry recently provided these figures for the country as a whole:

Job	Average Cost	Recovered on Resale
Remodeled kitchen	$16,500	75% to 125%
Remodeled bathroom	$ 4,900	50% to 100%
Room addition, 15 by 25	$28,000	40% to 75%

The figures in the table include remodeling jobs that were just luxuries. Many homeowners just got tired of their perfectly decent kitchens or bathrooms, or expanded an already commodious house. So the amount you may recover could be higher if your remodeling fixes a flaw in your house.

Among the mistakes to avoid: finishing a basement (most people don't like living underground), and turning a garage into a family room (unless it's near the kitchen, so a parent can keep an eye on the kids).

A horrendous mistake is to overimprove your house for your neighborhood and your community. If yours is a garden-variety house in a garden-variety area, don't expect to get your investment back on $30,000 black-walnut kitchen cabinets, or a bathroom with a $25,000 hot tub that turns itself on when you dial a certain phone number while you're away. People who can afford to buy houses with these gimmicks can also afford to live in Beverly Hills—and probably would prefer to.

But if a great many houses in your area have three or four bedrooms and yours has only two, another bedroom might be money in the bank.

Another horrendous mistake is remodeling so that yours winds up a "one-owner" house. No one else might want to live there because you've self-indulgently made the place *exactly* what you yourself want—from the eight-car garage for your antique automobiles to the special room for your toy-train sets.

One man I know paved over his backyard with blacktop; he simply hated mowing and weeding the lawn that had been there before. After trying to unload the place for months, he had the blacktop removed and the area reseeded for grass. So, unless you're fabulously wealthy and can afford to remove such indulgences before you sell, forget them.

There's yet another reason to consider remodeling. You might end up deciding not to sell. A benefit of staying put that you might overlook is that the exemption from taxes of $125,000 of your capital gains is for one time only. If you're 55 or over, you might want to hoard your opportunity and not move more than you absolutely have to.

Questions you should ask yourself:

☐ Do you like your neighbors now?
☐ Is your house close enough to your church or synagogue, to good schools, to shopping and recreation, to public transportation, to your job?

21

- ☐ Are the neighborhood and the community stable, or might they start deteriorating?
- ☐ Is your house sound to begin with, or are there fundamental flaws—small rooms, sweltering heat in summer and icy drafts in winter, a damp basement—that should persuade you to sell?

But bear in mind that remodeling can be an even more wearying experience than selling your house and buying another one. There may be bitter family battles over proper precedence in using available bathrooms. And while many remodelers (also called "general contractors") are conscientious and competent, almost everyone who has remodeled gripes about delays, overcharging, shoddy materials, and careless workmanship.

So now we have two reasons to remodel: to remedy a fault in your house before you sell, and perhaps as an alternative to selling altogether, even without an agent.

IF YOU DECIDE TO REMODEL . . .

Accept two facts beforehand.

- ☐ Remodeling will cost more than you estimate.
- ☐ Remodeling will take longer than you estimate.

Still, you may wind up enjoying yourself. "We had a guy add a room onto our house," says a physician's wife. "He was wonderful, but the only people he had helping him were a drug addict who happened to be his brother-in-law, and another yo-yo. He ended up working alone, and it took six months for him, working every day, to finish. The plus side was that he was good at taking phone messages and baby-sitting with the kids. We got used to having him around. We're thinking of other remodeling projects now, just to get him back. Even the dog misses him."

Your first step is to gather your family together and settle on exactly what projects should be done, and in what order. Usually the big messy jobs before the cosmetic ones, so the former don't damage the latter.

If your remodeling will be extensive and expensive—$25,000 and up—consider hiring an architect, advises Doug Walter of Denver, an architect who specializes in remodeling. Even if the cost is less than $25,000, think of hiring an architect for any remodeling job that will alter the front of your house and thus affect the house's salability. An architect may charge 10 to 15 percent of the cost, or a fee of $50 to $100 an hour. Phone a local branch of the American Institute of Architects for the names of any nearby who have done remodeling work.

If you can't afford an architect, or an architect isn't called for, consider other designers. An interior designer should belong to the American Society of Interior Designers. But be wary of an interior designer if your project calls for actual remodeling—altering the structure of a house.

A kitchen designer is ideally a CKD (Certified Kitchen Designer), accredited by the National Kitchen and Bath Association. Usually such a designer is employed by stores selling kitchen and bath equipment. But be skeptical of any who are paid commissions for what they sell you—say, half the price of all the cabinets you spring for. You may end up with more cabinets than you need.

Many remodeling firms have their own designers, but independent designers are usually the better choice. Kris Hallam, a medical-journal editor who has spent four years and $50,000 renovating a four-story brownstone in Brooklyn, New York, reports: "We had a big, well-respected Brooklyn firm that sells kitchen units 'design' the kitchen in our building's apartment. We paid a bit more, just for their 'vast expertise.' Well, after we went ahead with it, the darn refrigerator didn't fit! And all we got when we complained was a shrug. We had to sell the refrigerator and get a smaller one because the designer had measured wrong."

Still, R. Clayborne Porter, Jr., of Anchorage, an architect who does remodeling, grants that his chief competitor has a good designer on staff and a good architect on call. So don't rule out in-house designers entirely.

For a customized design by mail, complete with cost estimate, check out The Room Designer, P.O. Box 242, Route 5, Herkimer, NY 13350. A planning kit costs $18.95; the designs, $165.

When you work with a designer, read the remodeling magazines and clip illustrations of what you like. But don't fall for just a pretty face. "So many of the kitchens you see in magazines," Arthur Watkins warns, "would be the pits to work in. The sink, the refrigerator, and the range just aren't close enough together."

Wherever you get your designs, try to have an architect glance over them, for a reduced fee.

ESTIMATING THE COST

For a rough idea of what a remodeling job should cost, ask real-estate agents or banks in your area what square or cubic footage in a new house sells for. The cost of an addition will run 10 to 25 percent above the same space in a new house (reasons: the expense of ripping out the old materials and carting them away, and the inconvenience of working around the family). Converting existing space to another use costs only half to two-thirds the price of new space (because the necessary structure—of the attic, porch, whatever—is already there).

BE YOUR OWN GENERAL CONTRACTOR?

Should you go it alone, hiring subcontractors like electricians, carpenters, and plumbers, and supervising their work? It can save you the 10 to 20 percent that a general contractor would charge.

But you must be cool and efficient, have lots of time and patience, and know trustworthy tradespeople. Otherwise, you may wind up with an electrician who complains she can't do a good job because the painter fouled up, or a tile-layer who complains that he can't retile because the electrician, who arrived later than scheduled, is still busy with the bathroom.

You'll also have to make sure you have workers' compensation insurance (ask your agent) and building permits; select and schedule the delivery of materials; check the zoning code to see whether (for example) a second-story addition must be set back farther from the street than the first floor; and study the building code (are you allowed to use plastic pipes for your plumbing?).

Says Kris Hallam: "There's no reason why you can't be the general contractor on a remodeling job if you're willing to play hardball with these bozos. And you have to be tough, or they'll really stick it to you. One guy tried to hit us with an extra $500 for fixing a fireplace, although the cost was included in the estimate! You'll also have to take some time off from work—or leave your keys with a neighbor so the workers can get in, and later change your locks."

Should you do any of the work yourself? The answer depends on your skills, your time, your strength, whether you will need special tools, and how interested you are. But certainly your family can paint walls, and cart out debris. It will cut costs a bit, and should give you and your family a feeling of satisfaction.

FINDING A GENERAL CONTRACTOR

In most states, anyone at all can set up shop as a general contractor. "A carpenter who has remodeled a room may buy himself a pickup truck and power saw, place a big ad in the Yellow Pages, and await your phone call to have your kitchen renovated," says a real-estate broker in the Midwest. "I attended my high school's twentieth reunion a few weeks ago, and all the guys I remember as hoods now call themselves 'general contractors.'"

If you don't take the effort to find a good general contractor, you may wind up with someone who works infuriatingly slowly, or who is just inexperienced or incompetent. You may also find you've hired someone who cannot run a business profitably. Some remodelers may offer you a miraculously low price—simply because they're desperate for money and plan on cutting costs by using cheap materials. Or they may not pay the subcontractors, as they're supposed to, and you might find yourself forced to pay them yourself or lose your house.

Here's just one horror story, from Shirley Fitzpatrick of Hillsdale, New Jersey:

> We picked a man from the Yellow Pages to remodel the bathroom. He had big advertisements and his own radio-

dispatched trucks. My husband ripped out all the fixtures before the plumber arrived. He wasn't there five minutes. Knock comes at the door, and it's the plumbing inspector. He had seen the truck, and knew that this plumber wasn't licensed in Hillsdale. He threw him off the job!

We had three little children then, and without that bathroom, we had to move in with relatives for two weeks. And we had a heckuva time getting a new plumber because no one wanted to step on the old one's toes. But the first plumber got us a second one, and the bill from the first plumber came anyway—and it was so high, we refused to pay. He wouldn't itemize it. We paid him what another plumber said the job was worth, and we wound up in court. We won, too!

Steps that Shirley should have taken:

☐ Obtain the names of remodelers who enjoy fine reputations in your community. Talk to friends and neighbors, bankers, architects, real-estate agents. Clay Porter suggests that you even ask new-building contractors, because they themselves may hate to do remodeling work but know good people. Drive around town looking for work in progress, introduce yourself to the owners, and ask how satisfied they are.

Contractors who enjoy outstanding reputations will go out of their way to safeguard their good names. "I'll come back ten years after a renovation job if the owners call me about a problem," says Patrick J. Distasio of Bloomfield, New Jersey, a remodeler who has won fifty-five state and national remodeling awards. "I do it just for the good-will."

Questions to ask people: Were the remodeler's estimates of both how long the job would take and how much it would cost pretty accurate? When they stored their materials, did they put them somewhere for your convenience—or for theirs? Did they clean up every night? Were they and their workers courteous and considerate? Did they warn you in plenty of time when the water or electricity would be cut off? Did the laborers work continuously—or did they knock off after a day or two, move to another job, and return a few days later? Did they use the exact materials they were supposed to?

□ Look for credentials. A good contractor will probably belong to either the National Association of Home Builders/National Remodeling Council, in Washington, D.C., or the National Association of the Remodeling Industry (NARI), in Arlington, Virginia. These groups offer excellent study programs. Membership indicates that the contractor has professional pride. And you will have a third party to complain to if you're not satisfied with the job.

□ Check out remodelers. Some bat .500—they have as many admirers as they have detractors. So, even if someone seems to have a good reputation, phone the local unit of the National Association of the Remodeling Industry, which may have a Better Contractors Bureau that keeps complaint records. Run names past your local Better Business Bureau and consumer-protection agencies.

□ Ask contractors that are under consideration for the names of their recent customers, and phone them. Phone the contractors' bankers, too. (If a contractor hesitates to give you a name, she may be in financial trouble.) Make sure they have an office with a phone, that they're not working out of the glove compartments of their cars. They should have a carpenter on staff, and perhaps electricians and plumbers as well. And they should have been in business for at least five years.

□ By and large, give the nod to someone who specializes. But remember that the remodeler whose reputation has been built on, say, kitchens may do a wretched job on his first bathroom.

□ In general, choose a big company over a small one. If a big company underestimates the true cost of one job or two, it can survive. A small company might be forced to make up for its mistake by gouging its next few customers.

□ Finally, never, never choose a contractor because he comes cheap. Says Patrick Distasio, "A very low estimate may mean bad materials and good workmen, good materials and bad workmen, or—worst of all—bad materials and bad workmen."

Clay Porter tells of a woman in Alaska who was informed, by an architect, that an addition to her house would cost $120,000. She somehow found a contractor who promised to do it for $55,000. He did $55,000 worth of work—and disappeared.

The NARI reports that more than 80 percent of the complaints it receives come from customers who "thought they were getting a bargain price."

GETTING BIDS

Settle on one contractor you have confidence in. Have her give you a bid, with the specifications (what supplies you will need, how much, and the brand names), knowing that these specs will be top drawer. Then have your other candidates submit bids based on the same specs.

If the job is costly—over $10,000, say—obtain three to six bids. If you decide to change the specs, quickly notify each bidder, in writing, before they submit their bids. Usually a contractor needs a week to prepare an offer.

Besides a low price, look for a warranty on the work done. Some contractors offer five-year warranties. The least you should accept is a year. Once you have the bids in hand, show the various prices to the contractor with the most glittering reputation, assuming that a few are lower than his. See if he will come down a bit. Of course, if two contractors with comparable shining reputations submit markedly different bids, choose the one whose bid is lower.

Some remodelers may propose a "cost-plus" contract, but be on your guard unless you're dealing with someone as honest as General Washington. A cost-plus contract means that their profit—typically 10 percent—depends on what the materials cost. But read your contract carefully. One physician learned that his contractor had purchased the most expensive materials just to swell his own profit, and had also included in his final bill, as costs, a $500 weekly salary for himself and $250 for his secretary!

If you opt for a cost-plus contract, set a fixed maximum and specify that, if the final cost is less, you will pocket the difference. Also insist that the contractor give you a bill marked "paid" for all materials, and a record of the time each worker put in.

THE CONTRACT

The best rule about contracts with remodelers is one that Patrick Distasio himself mentions: "Pay them slow."

Typical contracts call on you to pay one-third of the total price at the beginning, one-third halfway through the job, and one-third at the end. But it's far better to pay as little as you can up front.

"I'd worry if it's more than 10 percent," says Hollye Fisk of Dallas, an architect-turned-lawyer. "If it's more than 10 percent, the contractor may just pocket the money and walk away." Fisk suggests that you pay the contractor month by month, after checking the bills for materials and for the subcontractors. "Any reputable contractor who's not desperate for money will accept this arrangement," Fisk says. "It's standard in commercial construction." Fisk also proposes that you not pay any bills unless you receive statements from all subcontractors that they have been paid to date. Finally, hold back at least 15 percent of the total price until the job is totally finished, you have tested everything, and any mess has been cleaned up.

A good contract describes how debris will be removed and how often (every night is best); how house furnishings will be protected; what work you yourself will do; how changes will affect the cost; approximately when the work will begin and when it will be finished; what happens if you are unhappy and want to cancel the contract; and the protection you have against property liens the subcontractors might lodge against you if the remodeler hasn't paid them.

The contract should mention the plans and specs, and they should be appended to the contract itself. The remodeler should state that she has liability and workers' compensation insurance.

If you must obtain financing first, specify in writing that the contract will not take effect unless you obtain a loan at a particular interest rate within two weeks (or whenever).

Don't be timid about proposing changes in the contract offered to you. A conscientious remodeler will have no cause for complaint if your changes are fair.

31

WHILE WORK IS IN PROGRESS

During construction, check that the materials are exactly what they are supposed to be, and do it every working day. Don't rely on a building inspector to keep the workers honest. Says architect Doug Walter, "A building inspector just looks for gross errors, not whether the lumber is the cheap 'standard' or whether it's good 'commercial' grade."

Do some homework, too. Read articles and books about the kind of remodeling you are having done, so you know how to evaluate the work—such how sidings should be installed (the fittings should be tight).

FLOATING A LOAN

A home-improvement loan remains tax deductible, even under the 1986 tax-reform act, if it is secured by your first or second house.

Consider a second mortgage or a variant, a home-equity loan (sort of a revolving credit account). Refinancing your first may be more costly because of new closing charges. If you do seek a second mortgage, consider one with a fluctuating rate and a limit on how high the rate can climb: You will pay a little less interest, at least to begin with, and home-improvement loans tend to be for short periods compared to mortgages—usually 2 to 15 years.

Resist any temptation to borrow from your remodeler. You can usually get better terms from a conventional lender. Also investigate Federal Housing Administration (FHA) loans if you need less than $17,500; for the names of lenders, write to the Title 1 Loan Insurance

Program, 451 Seventh Street, S.W., Washington, D.C. 20410-8000.

Borrowing from your pension plan for home improvements may be the easiest route of all, but in that case, make sure the improvements will add significantly to your house's value.

TAX ANGLES

Because of the remodeling, you will need more homeowners' insurance. And your property taxes may increase. But there may be tax savings, too.

If a physician recommended, in writing, that you (say) install a swimming pool for your arthritis, you may be able to deduct the difference between the cost of the pool and how much it raised the value of your house if your total medical expenses exceed 7.5 percent of your adjusted gross income (your gross income minus things like contributions to a pension plan). Ask a real-estate appraiser for help. The difference goes under "Medical and Dental Expenses" on Schedule A of your tax form.

If you have kept good records of all your improvements, their cost can be added to the "basis" of your house when you sell and calculate your capital gains (see the next chapter). Even if you plan on taking the $125,000 exemption when you sell, these days, with climbing house prices, $125,000 may not cover your entire profit.

Especially if you had the right remodeling done by the right people.

THREE WAYS TO BYPASS CAPITAL-GAINS TAXES

3

Avoiding a real-estate agent's commission is fine. Avoiding Uncle Sam's cut is plain wonderful, especially these days, when long-term capital-gains taxes have risen (the term capital gains means the profit you make on an asset you own that has gone up in value).

Time was when long-term capital gains were taxed leniently (long term: you owned the asset for six months or more). But now they are being taxed like ordinary income—your salary, for instance.

If you sold your house in 1986, the highest rate you could have paid on your capital gains was 20 percent. In 1987, it's 28 percent. In 1988, you will also pay a maximum of 28 percent—or even 33 percent if you fall into a special tax bracket (for married couples filing a joint return, it's $71,900 to $149,250).

There are at least three ways to avoid paying taxes on the appreciation of your house.

1. Don't sell it. Keep living there, or rent it out. Your heirs will inherit it, and no one will ever pay capital-gains taxes on the appreciation.

2. Sell the house, and buy another one at least as expensive as the one you sold. That way, you defer paying any capital-gains taxes.

3. Apply the once-in-a-lifetime exclusion of $125,000 from your capital gains.

Let's examine the second and third possibilities in more detail.

You can postpone or defer paying taxes on the appreciation of your house after you sell it if:

□ you buy and occupy another home within two years before or after selling your old one. That is, if you buy a new home and wait two years *before* selling your old one, you still qualify.

□ the new home is as expensive or more expensive than your old one. (Otherwise, you will owe taxes on the difference.)

□ the homes you sold and bought are your main residences (not, for example, your summer homes).

You can keep deferring taxes this way over and over again. But you cannot use this tactic more than once in a two-year period. (Exception: If you must move because of a job change, and you meet the rules that would let you deduct your moving expenses.)

The word "defer" is misleading. It refers to the fact that the taxes you avoid *may* come back to haunt you. The "basis" (the cost for tax purposes) of your *new* house is reduced by whatever tax you avoided in buying the new house.

Let's say you sold a home and made a $50,000 profit. You bought a more expensive home—for $200,000. For tax purposes, its cost is considered $200,000 minus the $50,000 profit—$150,000. So, when you sell *that* house, you might finally have to pay taxes on the $50,000 of capital gains.

But remember the *first* way to avoid capital-gains taxes: if you die while owning your home the capital gains are forgiven, so you may wind up "deferring" your taxes forever.

Okay, I'll entertain some questions.

Q. *What was that about "basis"?*

When you sell a house, you don't use just your purchase price and sales price to figure your gain. You're allowed to add other costs to your purchase price and wind up with an "adjusted basis." That shrinks the capital gains.

Here's what else you can add to your purchase price:

☐ The cost of improvements—like permanent storm windows, new wiring and plumbing, a new furnace, replacing the roof, landscaping, new carpeting, siding, a fence, paving your driveway—but *not* repairs. Yes, I know, new wiring and a new roof seem like repairs. But the IRS seems to accept any big expenses as improvements. (See pp. 45–47 for a checklist of home improvements.)

□ The cost of appliances.

□ Legal fees associated with adding the improvements.

□ Real-estate commissions (yes, some buyers use brokers).

□ Assessments for local improvements, such as sidewalks.

□ Closing costs, like title insurance and legal fees.

But you must subtract the following, which will *lower* your original purchase price and thus boost your capital gains:

□ Any residential energy credits you deducted from your taxes.

□ Any casualty loss you deducted, which lowered the value of your property (for example, damage caused by a fire).

□ The gain postponed on the sale of an earlier home.

Now let's look at the "adjusted sales price." Here, you can deduct the following from the actual sales price:

□ Advertising expenses.

□ The cost of preparing a fact sheet.

□ Real-estate commissions (heaven forbid!).

□ Legal fees, maps, geological surveys, recording fees, termite inspection, etc.

□ Loan charges, such as "points" the seller in rare instances might have to pay. (A "point" is 1 percent of the amount of a mortgage.)

□ Fix-up expenses—for decorating or repair work during the 90 days before you sell your home, and paid for within 30 days after the sale. (You can't deduct the value of your own labor, though.)

Q. *Is it true that I can deduct fix-up expenses from my sale price only if I don't buy a more expensive home?*

Yes. If you buy a home as expensive or more expensive, all your gain is postponed—so fix-up expenses don't matter.

Q. *Can I deduct any loss if my house has declined in value?*

No, not unless you were renting out the house. But you will have to persuade the IRS that the house was being rented permanently, not temporarily—that you didn't just go through the motions of renting it out, to deduct the loss.

Q. *I don't want to buy a more expensive home. I'm getting on in years, and want fewer rooms to clean. What can I do?*

Move to a more expensive but smaller home—say, in Beverly Hills. Or just buy a smaller home with a lot more land, to push up the price. You can also buy a house, then—within two years before or after selling your old one—add improvements, like a swimming pool. These improvements will serve to boost your purchase price. Finally, you can use the $125,000 exemption, explained in detail on page 42.

Q. *I bought my house for $50,000, and it's now worth $100,000. If I don't sell it, but exchange it for another that's equal in value, can I defer the tax on the gain?*

Yes, an exchange is considered a sale.

Q. *What if I buy and move into a houseboat, trailer, condo, or co-op, or a yacht? Can I defer my gain?*

Yes. And congratulations on the yacht.

Q. *Is it all right if my replacement home is not in this country?*

Yes.

Q. *I lost the sales slips on my improvements. Am I out of luck?*

Maybe not. You can use building permits, canceled checks, even before-and-after photos of your house to prove you made improvements, and thus add their cost to the basis of your house. Or you may be able to demonstrate the value of your improvements from yearly property-tax records.

Q. *I'm having a new home built. Does it qualify as a replacement residence?*

Yes.

Q. *I'm in the armed forces. Do I have to abide by the two-year rule?*

Maybe not. If your tax home is outside this country, the rule may be suspended. Check with your tax adviser.

Q. *The house I was about to move into burned down, so I had to wait to move in. I don't meet the two-year test now. Am I out of luck?*

Yes. You must buy and *occupy* the home. The IRS is unrelenting about this. No excuses, like "The builders didn't finish my new house when they were supposed to."

Q. *When I sold my house, I moved more than 35 miles away, to be closer to my new job. Should I deduct costs like appraisal fees as moving expenses or add them to the basis of my new home?*

Generally, deduct them as moving expenses, if you itemize, because you'll get the deductions more quickly.

Q. *Should I ever try* not *to buy a replacement home within two years of selling my old home?*

Yes, if you have large losses to offset the gains. Only $3,000 of these losses can be subtracted from ordinary income (your salary) every year. But if you can subtract the losses in full from the capital gains on the sale of a home, then these gains will not lower the basis of your new house.

Q. *I sold my house for $80,000 (adjusted sales price), with a $10,000 gain. I bought a new house for $75,000 (the adjusted basis). Do I owe taxes on the $10,000 gain? Or on the $5,000 that cannot be deferred?*

Good question. You can choose whichever is less—in this case, $5,000. The other $5,000 reduces the basis of your new home.

Q. *How about an example of all these calculations?*

Here's one the IRS provides:

Your home has a basis of $45,000. You sell it for $61,400. Selling expenses were $5,000. You spent $900 on new blinds and a new water heater. You also spent $800 on painting the inside and outside of your home—and had the work done within 90 days of the sale, paying the bill within 30 days after the sale.

1.	Selling price of old home:	$61,400
2.	Minus selling expenses:	5,000
3.	Amount realized:	56,400
4.	Basis of old home:	45,000
5.	Add improvements (blinds, heater):	900
6.	New basis of old home:	45,900
7.	Gain on old home (line 3 minus line 6):	10,500

You buy and occupy another home that cost $54,600 within two years of selling your old one. Now you can postpone paying taxes on most of the $10,500. Here are the calculations:

8. Amount realized (line 3): $56,400
9. Minus fix-up expenses (painting):   800
10. Adjusted sales price: 55,600
11. Cost of replacement home: 54,600
12. Gain *not* postponed
    (line 10 minus line 11):   1,000
13. Gain postponed
    (line 7 minus line 12):   9,500
14. Cost of new home (line 11):   54,600
15. Minus gain postponed (line 13):   9,500
16. Adjusted basis of new home: 45,100

Note that fix-up expenses may *not* be deducted from the profit of the sale of a home. But they can reduce the amount you realize (line 8) and thus boost the amount you can postpone *if you buy a less expensive house* (as you did here).

Besides the deferral option, you can subtract $125,000 from your capital gains if:

☐ you or your spouse were 55 when your house was sold
☐ the house was your main residence
☐ you or your spouse lived there for three of the five years before you sold it

You can use the $125,000 exclusion only once in your lifetime.
Question time.

42

Q. *Which should I choose, the deferral or the exclusion?*

In general, choose the deferral. You can use it over and over again. At some later time, you might be better off using the exclusion. Of course, you can use both—shield $125,000 from taxes, postpone taxes on whatever gain is over $125,000.

Q. *I made a mistake. I used the exclusion to shield $50,000 of gain. Now I'm selling again, but I have $120,000 of gain to protect. Can I revoke my previous exclusion?*

Yes, you have three years from the date your old return was due to be filed to revoke that exclusion.

Q. *You mean I can't use $50,000 now, and $75,000 of the exclusion later on?*

You got it. You must use the exclusion all at once.

Q. *If one spouse is 55, and the other 25, do they qualify for the exclusion?*

Yes, if the house is owned jointly. And if the older spouse has died (but not before living in the house three of the five years before the sale), the survivor will still qualify.

Q. *Can I take the exclusion even if I've been renting the house?*

Yes, if you've been renting it for two years, and lived there for the previous three years.

Q. *I married a 60-year-old widow, and I'm 62. She has used the $125,000 before. Can she and I still use the $125,000 exclusion on our new house?*

No, you cannot even exclude half, $62,500.

Q. *I recently married a widow, too. But she's only 50, not 55. She owns the house. If she sells it, can she use the $125,000 exclusion because I'm over 55?*

No, not unless you become a joint owner and live in the house for three years.

Q. *I'll be 55 later in the year. If I sell now, do I qualify for the exclusion?*

No. Usually the IRS holds that your age on December 31 is your age for the entire year, but with regard to the exclusion, you must actually be 55 when you sell.

Q. *How about an example of the calculations?*

All right. You're 60, and sell your main residence for $400,000. The basis of this residence is $75,000.

1. Selling price of old home:		$400,000
2. Basis of old home:		- 75,000
3. Gain:		325,000
4. Exclusion:		-125,000
5. Taxable gain:		200,000

Now, let's combine the exclusion with the deferral. You buy a new house for $300,000.

5. Taxable gain (after exclusion):		$200,000
6. Price of new home:		-300,000
7. Taxable gain (line 5 minus line 6)		0
8. Basis of new home (line 6 minus line 5)		100,000

Yes, tax computations can be complicated, and even an independent-minded, resourceful fizzbo may need a tax adviser.

CHECKLIST OF HOME IMPROVEMENTS

You can lower the taxes you may owe on any capital gains from the sale of your house by adding the cost of improvements to the original price you paid for your house. This list can help you recall any improvements—these are *not* repairs—you made.

IMPROVEMENTS TO THE HOUSE

Structural work

☐ Work done on the foundation to eliminate water seepage and settling

☐ Upgrading of interiors, such as installation or improvement of fireplace with major brick, stone, cement, or plastering work

☐ New doors, new windows, or acoustic ceilings

☐ Installation of louvers and screen vents in the attic

☐ Strengthening of the house's structure with steel girders, reinforcing rods, or floor jacks

☐ Upgrading of roofing, gutters, or exterior covering of house

☐ Installation of awnings, sunshades, shutters, blinds, storm doors, storm windows, or screens

Equipment

☐ Sauna

☐ Intercoms

☐ Elevator

☐ Built-in stereo equipment or hobby machinery

☐ Additional stoves

☐ Fire or burglar alarms

☐ Built-in freezer or refrigerator

☐ Garbage disposal or dishwasher

Additions and finishing
☐ Closets, laundry chutes, or dumbwaiters
☐ Attic and basement improvements
☐ Porches
☐ Rooms

Built-in furnishings
☐ Installation of permanent floor covering
☐ Addition of permanently placed units, such as chests, cabinets or shelving

Plumbing, heating, and air conditioning
☐ Upgrading of heating systems
☐ New or additional plumbing fixtures, sinks, laundry tubs, or water softeners
☐ Installation of air-conditioning units, a central air-conditioning system, attic fans, air humidifiers and de-humidifiers, or air-filtration systems
☐ Piping, tanks, pumps, or wells

Electrical wiring
☐ Additional outlets or switches
☐ Installation of new power lines or lighting fixtures

IMPROVEMENTS TO THE GROUNDS

Landscaping
☐ Addition or redesign of decorative pools or arbors
☐ Addition or removal of trees or shrubbery
☐ Enlargement of lawn area
☐ Resurfacing of land areas or installation of drain tiles or other equipment to eliminate problems associated with the property's water drainage

Equipment
- [ ] Underground sprinkler system
- [ ] Outdoor sound systems, lighting, or lampposts
- [ ] Barbecue pits or incinerators

Paving and surfaces
- [ ] Laying or extension of walks or curbs
- [ ] Addition or enlargement of patios
- [ ] Blacktopping or other improvements to driveway

Recreational facilities
- [ ] Children's playground equipment
- [ ] Installation of an outdoor swimming pool as well as other, related facilities
- [ ] Tennis, badminton, or other game courts

Structures
- [ ] Improvement of garages, carports, tool sheds, stables, barns, greenhouses, or other outbuildings
- [ ] Addition or removal of fences, walls, or trellises

47

THE RIGHT PRICE
SELLS A HOUSE

WHICH IS WORSE: DRASTICALLY
OVERPRICING OR UNDERPRICING
A HOUSE?

4

Underpricing is probably worse. If
you overprice a house, you may get
lucky and sell it. Or you may eventually come to your senses, lower the
price, and sell the place for a more
reasonable figure. But if you underprice your house, you automatically lose money you could have
made.

Bear in mind that the value of your
house is not set in stone. The price a
house sells for depends in large part
on what a buyer can afford and how
closely the house fulfills the buyer's

needs and dreams. That's why Charles Atwood, president of Sotheby International Realty in New York City, which sells expensive houses (average, $600,000), claims that estimating the value of a house is as much an art as a science. And Arlen C. Mills of Orinda, California, a professional appraiser, confesses, "I can't tell you whether my own condo is worth $310,000 or $325,000—and I'm an expert!"

In putting a price tag on your house, you may err on the side of optimism. The market is brisk, it's spring, your place is a "cream puff" (generally meaning a desirable home), and you can take your sweet old time about selling it. So you might add 15 percent to the "probable selling price."

Alas, your house may sit—and sit and sit. Buyers may become worried when they learn how long you have been trying to unload the place. Is there something wrong with it? Was it the subject of a film about a house inhabited by demons? Would they have the same trouble if they tried to sell it? You yourself may become weary of showing your house, tired of open houses, and disgusted with paying for newspaper ads. So, depressed and discouraged, you drastically reduce your price. "If you have to lower the original price," says James W. Klopfenstein, president of the Society of Real Estate Appraisers, "typically you will realize less than if the property had been priced right, at the beginning." Reason: Houses that have been on the market a while lose a little of their appeal.

On the other hand, you might err on the side of caution. Perhaps you must move quickly, the market is sluggish, it's the dead of winter, and—like my own house—yours has old-fashioned avocado-colored appliances and a master bedroom with one measly closet.

So you offer the house at what you consider a very reasonable figure.

Alas, you may have drastically underpriced your house. It sells very quickly. The first weekend, several people may bid for it, offering full price. There may even be a spontaneous auction: Buyers exceed your offering price. True, you wind up moving quickly; you no longer have to hang around the house waiting for phone calls and for visitors; you don't have to escort a stream of strangers through your bedrooms. But for the remainder of your life you may be tormented by the thought— Could I have sold it for more?

Any house that sells in a weekend could be cause for concern. Still, it may just have been a fluke: The ideal buyer just happened along right then instead of three or six months later.

WHICH IS MORE COMMON—AND WHY?

"Overpricing is the norm rather than the exception," says Klopfenstein. Reasons:

□ Some homeowners are greedy. I once checked out a fine house, and offered $37,000. (This was probably before you were born.) The owner was about to list with a broker. He seemed insulted by my offer, and never got back to me. He listed with the broker, offered the house for $41,000, and sold it for $37,000. The seller thus lost 7 percent of his money—$2,590, the broker's commission. (Yes, I've been gloating ever since.)

□ Some homeowners are misinformed. Through the grapevine they have heard that a house similar to theirs went for $120,000. But that house may actually have sold for much less—sellers don't like spreading the word that their houses don't go for the asking price. Or, if the figure was correct, the seller may have helped out the buyer with a low-interest mortgage, or simply found someone unfamiliar with local prices. (In California, brokers call such a person "a buyer from the East.") It's also possible that our homeowner doesn't recognize the flaws in her own house—the small bedrooms, the sparse and tiny closets, the irregularly shaped lot, etc.

□ Many homeowners overvalue the improvements they have made—the outdoor deck, the enclosed porch, the paneled basement (see Chapter 2). Some improvements, in fact, may reduce the value of a home—a swimming pool, for example, particularly in the North, where the swimming season is short. I once refused even to look at a reasonably priced house with a pool simply because I loathed the idea of maintaining it, especially when there was an attractive municipal pool nearby.

Besides, as Klopfenstein points out, an improvement usually costs more if it is added onto an existing house than if it had been built along with the house itself. So, on the market, it isn't worth nearly as much as you paid. A spare room may cost $28,000; on the market, competing with other homes with the same room, it may be worth only $12,000. "Cost," says Klopfenstein, "does not always create value."

□ Real-estate agents may deliberately overprice a house, especially if they know they are competing for a listing. If one agent tells you he can sell your house for $115,000, and another says $110,000, it's human nature for you to go with the agent who seems to be confident she can get you $5,000 more. Actually, such agents plan to talk you down either *before* the house goes on the market or *after* it has sat for a while and you have been humbled.

And then there are people who drastically underprice their houses. Reasons:

□ They cannot believe their houses have appreciated so much. I recall looking at a house selling for $71,900. Two kitchens, a fireplace that occupied almost an entire wall, four entrance closets, floor-to-ceiling windows in the living room, and so forth. The owners—two elderly sisters—had lived there for 30 years; they never imagined that their $15,000 house could now be worth almost five times as much. I was the very first buyer to see it, and offered $69,900. While I was waiting for a response, three other buyers offered $71,900, and one walked off with it. (The lesson I learned: Don't bargain over a bargain.)

□ Agents may talk sellers into underpricing their homes. One might think, offhand, that agents would prefer that sellers garner the highest sale price possible, so they themselves get a bigger cut. But a listing agent (the one you sign up with) always gets a percentage of the commission, typically half; the rest goes to the agent who brings in a "ready, willing, and able" buyer. If the listing agent can sell the house, too, she gets the entire commission. And with an underpriced house, the listing agent has a splendid chance of selling it before other agents who belong to the multiple-listing service.

Besides, clever agents are aware that money up front is more valuable than money three to six months from now. A quick sale also means no schlepping buyers around, showing the house again and again, dickering with buyer and seller over the price. The most successful agents—those who write books with titles like How I Made a Million Selling Real Estate—concentrate their efforts on underpriced houses, to make the most profitable use of their time.

One agent has even described how she persuades sellers to accept her figure. Let's suppose she believes that a house should be listed at $89,000. She gives the sellers a figure of $87,000. They moan and grumble. So she pretends to be persuaded to "raise" the price to $89,000—and, pleased with this "concession," the sellers go along.

An agent who knows you are not asking other agents to evaluate your house may be more likely to give you an unrealistically low estimate.

Of course, a few agents persuade sellers to underprice their houses because they want to sell the houses to friends or accomplices. This is cause for their licenses to be revoked.

SHOULD AN AGENT SET THE PRICE OF YOUR HOUSE?

No. Thou shalt never ask only one agent to estimate the market value of your home. You should ask a minimum of three—and, to be on the safe side, half a dozen.

Don't feel guilty about using their time. If you ever decide to list your house with a broker, you can choose among the agents who gave you a price estimate. Or, if you're also buying locally, you can use the agent who impressed you the most.

When the agents arrive (separately, of course), use the opportunity to pick their brains. Ask them:

□ What's the residential real-estate market like now?
□ What changes would they recommend that you make in your house?

☐ What do they like most about your house? What drawbacks do they see?

☐ What newspapers are best to advertise in? What days of the week?

☐ Do they know any good real-estate lawyers?

☐ If you listed your house with them, would they give you a break on the commission?

☐ Which local banks are the most generous with mortgage money?

All right, three agents inspect your house and give you estimates of $83,000, $85,000, and $90,000. The average: $86,000.

Now, the agents would probably go on to suggest that you pad their price estimates, for bargaining. Usually that means 5 to 10 percent more. But don't forget that you may save a 6 or 7 percent broker's commission. If you sell at $86,000, you would be paying a commission of $5,160 to $6,020. Your getaway price would be about $80,500.

What you might do: Aim at getting away with $85,000, so you get the lion's share of the commission. (After all, you, not the buyer, are doing most of the work.) You might offer the house at $89,990, planning to come down to $85,000. Of course, your decision will be influenced by how the real-estate market is faring, and whether you are eager to sell quickly or you are willing to take your time.

To be on the safe side, you might offer the house at $87,900, preparing to sell for $83,500. That way you would split the commission with the buyer—and be more assured of selling your home within a fairly short time. Your probable extra profit would be $83,500 minus $80,500, or $3,000.

SHOULD YOU USE A REAL-ESTATE APPRAISER TO SET THE PRICE OF YOUR HOUSE?

Not usually. If yours is the typical house, you can get away with the minimum-of-three-agents approach.

Appraisers, after all, charge $200-$275 to evaluate the average house. And their estimates are sometimes on the conservative side. To arrive at a price for your house, they may look at similar houses that were sold six months ago, and not make an adjustment for rising prices (although they are supposed to). Besides, all the best professionals tend to be conservative—doctors, lawyers, writers. That may be why homeowners are disappointed by appraisals. (Of course, you can always argue with the appraiser or raise the selling price yourself.)

There are advantages to using an appraiser, though. James Klopfenstein grants that it *may* be "the party line," but appraisers tend to be more objective than real-estate agents. (Arlen Mills, however, thinks an experienced, conscientious agent would do as well.) And appraisers generally are more competent than real-estate agents. They may examine not just the recent selling prices of houses like yours; they may also consider the value of the land and the cost of rebuilding your house on that land. Also, a formal appraisal will enable a bank to tell you the size of the mortgage it will give on your home.

So it's six of one and half a dozen of the other. Calling in three agents one by one takes more time; an appraiser costs money. On balance, it's probably better to have various agents estimate the value of your house, provided you use the opportunity to learn from them.

But there's an important exception. Hire an appraiser,

as Klopfenstein suggests, if your house is unusual—unusual in design or unusual for the setting or neighborhood, or larger, or boasts more amenities. In such a case, real-estate agents may not be able to give you as accurate a "probable sales price" as an appraiser can.

To find an appraiser, ask the holder of your mortgage to suggest names. At the same time, ask whether the mortgage holder will let you know how much of a mortgage it will grant a buyer, based on the appraisal.

The better appraisers belong to the American Institute of Real Estate Appraisers or the Society of Real Estate Appraisers, both of which are in Chicago. Make sure any appraiser you hire has such credentials.

WHO SHOULD MAKE THE FINAL DECISION ON PRICE?

Whether you call in agents or hire an appraiser to price your house, you yourself should help make the final decision. Says Stuart Siegel, a vice-president of Sotheby International Realty: "It should be a shared decision."

Check the newspaper ads for prices of houses in your area. Ask friends and neighbors who recently moved in, or out, what their houses sold for. Visit a broker's office and ask to look at "comparatives"—houses like yours that were sold recently. Visit a few houses for sale. (A side benefit: You'll get some ideas about sprucing up your house and how to show it to buyers.)

SHOULD A HOMEOWNER WAIT UNTIL SPRING TO SELL—TO GET THE BEST PRICE?

Not necessarily. Appraiser Mills argues that a house is worth the same in January as in April—it just may take five months to sell in January, three months in April. Besides, even in winter, there are live buyers out there. And the faster you sell your house, the more time you will have to look for a new one.

Still, as a concession to the seasons, you might run ads only occasionally in the winter, and in the spring go for a blitz of ads.

SHOULD YOU TELL BUYERS ABOUT THE MULTIPLE MURDERS?

5

If you are harboring either of the following misconceptions, expunge them from your mind immediately:

1. The rule of *caveat emptor* (let the buyer beware) is still sacred. (A judge once explained this rule as follows: If a buyer doesn't look before he leaps, "it is his folly, against which the law, that encourages no negligence, will give him no relief.")

2. If the buyer signs a contract agreeing to buy your house "as is," he has no legal recourse later if he finds flaws.

Now, etch *this* into your mind:

If you fail to disclose a significant defect in your house, one that is not obvious, you could wind up in a mess of trouble. The sale could be canceled. A court may order you to pay for repairing the defect. A court may even sock you with "punitive" damages—a fine (punishment) to teach you to behave yourself in the future.

So, if there is a major flaw in your house or property that a buyer cannot easily see (the legal term is that it's "latent," not "patent"), fix it. Or, if you cannot afford to fix it, or it's unfixable (your house is in a flood plain), level with the buyer. Have witnesses that you warned him. You might even put it in the contract—"The buyer is aware that this house is in an area designated as a flood plain."

No, you need not worry about anything minor, such as a gas stove for which you have to use matches because it doesn't light automatically. You need not worry about anything that buyers can plainly see: the cracks in the plaster ceiling, the avocado-colored appliances. And an "as is" contract cannot hurt you. If you ever wind up in court, you can argue that this provision should have prompted the buyer to inspect the house and grounds as thoroughly as possible (but do see, on page 64, the case of The Seller Who Didn't Tell the Buyer that His House Had Been Condemned).

You will get a good idea from the following actual court cases what you should worry about.

THE CASE OF THE MULTIPLE MURDERS

R bought a house in California for $76,000. The seller, K, and the seller's agent deliberately didn't tell R that, ten years earlier, a woman and her four children had been

60

murdered in the house. K even asked neighbors not to apprise R of the murders.

But one gossipy neighbor did tell R. And R hired an appraiser, who informed her that, because of the house's horrible history, it was worth only $65,000.

R sued—both for damages and to cancel the sale. A lower court threw out her suit, arguing that if such an "irrational" consideration were permitted to vitiate a sale the entire real-estate market would be in turmoil.

R appealed. And, on appeal, she was permitted to pursue her suit. The court held:

> The critical question is: does the seller have a duty to disclose here? Resolution of this question depends on the materiality of the fact of the murders. In general . . . : "where the seller knows of facts *materially* affecting the value or desirability of the property which are known or accessible only to him and also knows that such facts are not known to, or within the reach of the diligent attention and observation of, the buyer, the seller is under a duty to disclose them to the buyer." . . .
>
> Should this variety of ill-repute be required to be disclosed? . .
>
> The paramount argument against an affirmative conclusion is it permits the camel's nose of unrestrained irrationality admission to the tent. If such an "irrational" consideration is permitted as a basis of [canceling a sale,] the stability of all [such sales] will be seriously undermined. Any fact that might disquiet the enjoyment of some segment of the buying public may be seized upon by a disgruntled purchaser to void a bargain.
>
> [But in] our view, keeping this genie in the bottle is not as difficult a task as these arguments assume. [R's complaints are clearly *not*] peripheral, insubstantial, or fancied harms.

The court went on to say that a house's reputation does have a bearing on its value:

> Reputation and history can have a significant effect on the value of realty. "George Washington slept here" is worth some-

> thing . . . . Ill-repute or "bad will" conversely may depress the value of property . . . .
> Whether [R] will be able to prove her allegation that the decade-old multiple murder has a significant effect on market value, we cannot determine. If she is able to do so by competent evidence, she is entitled to a favorable ruling on the issues of materiality and duty to disclose . . .

The woman won a sizable settlement, and proceeded to rent the house (first telling the buyers, of course, about the murders).

Lesson: Let buyers know if your house has a shady history. Psychologically, though, it may be wiser to wait until they have fallen in love with your home before telling them, say, that it's haunted.

THE SELLER WHO DIDN'T NOTICE NOAH'S FLOOD

In Illinois, C bought a house from H. A month later, C received a letter from her mortgage lender advising her that her home was in a flood-hazard area, and she would need flood insurance in order to obtain a mortgage.

C sued to have the sale canceled, claiming that the seller had not warned her that she needed flood insurance—or that the entire area was so badly flooded during heavy rains that her house became "inaccessible."

The seller, for his part, said he knew nothing about flooding or flood-insurance requirements. He then went on to say that the buyer should have known: A government map showed that the property was in a flood zone, so it was a matter of public record!

A lower court threw out the complaint, but an appeals court reversed the decision. The appeals court held that, while the Federal Insurance Administration had published a map showing that the property was in a flood zone, this wasn't "the type of information an average prospective buyer would research if given no indication whatsoever that flooding was a problem."

As regards the seller's contention that he was unaware that the area sank so far beneath water during heavy rains that no one could even reach the house, the court seemed a trifle skeptical.

THE CASE OF THE SURPRISE WITNESS

In Pittsburgh, a family inspected a vacant house. In the basement, they noticed a discolored area on the wall near the sewage pipe. Was the sewer system working well? The seller's agent said he knew of no problems.

The family bought the house and moved in. Two weeks later, the sewage pipe backed up, filling their basement with slime, excrement, and toilet paper. The cost of the repair was $2,400. Still, the odor remained so overpowering that the family asked relatives to care for their baby for a while.

In court, the broker and the seller claimed they knew nothing of a sewage problem.

But, luckily, the family's lawyer was able to find a fellow who had been renting the house some while back. And this fellow readily testified that, on many different occasions, he had told the broker that the basement was flooded with sewage. In fact, *he* had moved out to escape the odor.

The broker and the seller had to pay the $2,400 bill.

THE CASE OF THE MISCONSTRUCTED HOUSE

You need not find a surprise witness to prove that a fraud has occurred.

63

In Illinois, M inspected a house and noticed a large pool of water in the basement. The water, said the broker, was caused by a leaky valve on the sump pump, which would soon be fixed. M bought the property.

But even after he moved in, M noticed water in the basement. He sued—and won.

But wasn't the water problem "patent" (obvious) and not "latent" (hidden)?

A court noted that an engineer reported that the house had been built with its foundation lower than the level of ground water. So, said the court, "We do not believe that because [M] saw sump pumps in the basement, or noticed the leaking in the northwest corner wall, [he was made aware] that the home was improperly built."

Now, the seller, V, had admitted to M that there was some leakage in the basement, and he had mentioned that the sump pumps had to be fixed. Did he really not know how bad the situation was?

Ruled the court: "Evidence at the trial showed that defendant [V] was involved in the construction of the residence, that he lived there for at least two and a half years, and that there were traces of water damage to boxes and a stairwell when the property was put up for sale. It was also undisputed that V had ample opportunity to notice a chronic water problem in the basement."

Circumstantial evidence thus proved the seller guilty of fraud.

THE SELLER WHO DIDN'T TELL THE BUYER THAT HIS HOUSE HAD BEEN CONDEMNED!

Why should he? argued the seller. His contract had an "as is" clause. The buyer had agreed to purchase the property "in its present state and condition," and the contract specified that no "representations, guarantees or warranties of any kind" had been made. In other words, the seller had not lied about what miserable shape the property was in, or that it had been condemned. He just hadn't volunteered the information.

A trial court found for the defendant, but on appeal this was reversed.

Said the appeals court: "A provision in a contract of sale that the buyer takes the property in the condition in which it is, or 'as is,' does not necessarily confer on the seller general immunity from liability from fraud." An "as is" provision, said the court, may cover something visible, like a dilapidated stairway, but not "a subterranean creek in the backyard or an unexploded bomb buried in the basement . . . known to the seller."

Sellers have also landed up in court for not disclosing termite damage; claiming that a house had a sophisticated septic-tank system when it had a cesspool (a mere hole in the ground); not volunteering the fact that home improvements had been made without a building permit and were thus in violation of zoning codes; and not revealing that a house had been built on "filled" ground, causing the walls and foundation to crack.

Very recent cases should persuade sellers to become even more open and frank with buyers. For example, an Alaskan court has held a seller liable for telling a buyer an untruth, even though the seller thought he was being truthful. (The seller had assured a buyer that a well on his land could produce water sufficient for washing and drinking—but was wrong.) As the court held: "Owners are presumed to know the character and attributes of the land conveyed, and buyers are consequently entitled to rely on the seller's reasonable representations."

These very recent cases also seem to be eroding the difference between "latent" and "patent" defects. A good example is the sump pump case: Even though the buyer spotted sump pumps at work and saw water in the basement, he did not know how serious the problem was.

Thus, in the housing market, the pendulum seems to be swinging away from the old rule of *caveat emptor* to *caveat venditor*—let the seller beware.

No doubt homeowners who try to sell their houses without agents are somewhat more likely to conceal major defects. Even so, a lawyer for the National Association of Realtors has written, "All too often, real estate professionals neglect to tell the seller, starting at the listing presentation, that full disclosure about known or potential property problems is essential to avoid liability."

IS THERE A LAWYER IN THE HOUSE?

Lawyers I have known:

□ The trusted family lawyer who told me he would charge $200 to handle the closing, and at the closing itself presented me with a long, detailed bill for $500. ("I thought you had said $200," a much more youthful and timid version of myself whined. "I couldn't do it for less," he snapped.) Later that day, my wife's family broke the news to me: "You have to get everything he says in writing. You've got to watch him like a hawk."

I sent letters of complaint to national and local bar associations. A waste of time. The now-distrusted family lawyer then wrote to me that he had informed me about the $500 charge—and had also informed me he was getting a commission from the title insurance he had obtained on my behalf. That was also news. Obviously, he was putting it in writing to protect himself, in case I ever learned about that kickback.

□ The high school friend who became a lawyer. I wanted to pay him his full fee, but he magnanimously insisted on charging the minimum. So he did slipshod work, unconsciously resenting the fact that he was charging me so little. Also, he didn't show up for the closing—and didn't have anyone covering for him. Closing postponed. Broker, seller, buyer, other lawyers mad. Rancor and recrimination all around.

□ The tough-as-nails lawyer. He was the seller's last-minute choice. The seller and I were getting along fabulously. I had purchased a cream puff at a bargain price. He had sold a lemon for an obscene profit. Then his lawyer arrived—young, suspicious, aggressive. (The law, someone has said, provides a socially acceptable career for all the psychopaths in our midst.) He glared at me, my wife, and my lawyer as if we were suing his client. He studied the certified check I handed over so intently and for such a long time that I thought he might wind up biting it. He carped over various parts of the contract, trying to win back chandeliers and fireplace equipment. A meeting that had begun harmoniously, in a party-like atmosphere, became grim and tense.

Everyone seems to have had sour experiences with lawyers. But if you're selling your house yourself, it's vital to hire a lawyer, and as early as possible. You can ask your lawyer whatever questions you might have asked a real-estate agent, and probably get more-informed answers.

Your lawyer can help you establish an offering price; suggest how much "earnest money" (a token payment to demonstrate the buyer's seriousness) you should demand; help with the price negotiation; provide a customized contract for you to keep in your home; qualify the buyer (check that she really has the wherewithal to purchase your home); help find a mortgage for the buyer; negotiate with the buyer's lawyer over what constitutes a fixture (which goes with the house) and what's a furnishing (which goes with you); prorate closing costs; and, in general, protect your interests.

"You're the good guy," says Mike McClintock, author of *Getting Your Money's Worth from Home and Real Estate Professionals*. "Your lawyer is the bad guy who insists on nitpicking details that serve your interest."

Lawyers come in two varieties: LLBs (bachelors of law) and JDs (doctors of law). There's no difference, although JDs are usually younger because that degree is more fashionable now.

Today, most lawyers are specialists, but they may not be eager to announce their specialties lest it cut down on their overall employment. (A cardinal failing of lawyers seems to be that they think they know virtually everything, including how you should invest your money.)

Communications between you and your lawyer are privileged.

Helping you sell your house is usually a job that most family lawyers can handle. Just check that your family lawyer has presided over a good many closings—and recent ones, too.

If you don't have a regular lawyer, hiring one to help

you sell your house is an excellent way to find one. Scouting around for a top-notch lawyer in an emergency, when you don't have time to spare, can be disastrous. A former president of the American Bar Association has estimated that 20 to 25 percent of all lawyers are incompetent. You don't want to retain the services of someone of that ilk the night a member of your family gets in trouble with the law.

Your first task is to obtain names. Ask your county bar association. Phone a nearby law school's department of administration. Speak to your accountant, banker, stockbroker, physician, clergy, friends, neighbors, and people who have recently sold or purchased houses. When one name pops up repeatedly, you're almost home—or out of your home.

Make sure that the people you ask for names have actually used the lawyer, and recently. A recommendation ("I used Jones, and he was great") counts more than a referral ("I've heard Smith's name mentioned a lot").

Questions to ask people who have used a particular lawyer:

☐ Were his fees reasonable?

☐ Did she warn you if estimated fees had to be raised?

☐ Is she fairly prosperous—or scrounging around for clients?

☐ Did he return your phone calls the same day, or the following day?

☐ Did you get what you wanted—the fireplace equipment, a refrigerator that was really new?

☐ Was he available at night, on weekends, on holidays? Did he at least have someone covering for him?

☐ Did she keep you informed? Send you copies of all

important documents?

☐ Did she level with you? Tell you what you may not have wanted to hear—such as, "Your house isn't selling because it's overpriced"?

☐ Does he know his way around town? Is he acquainted with local appraisers, bankers, judges?

☐ Did he make everything clear to you, or indulge in impenetrable legal jargon?

☐ Did she work fast?

☐ Would you hire her again, without hesitation?

☐ Was there anything at all you didn't like about the lawyer?

Once you have assembled a list of names, phone two or three of the lawyers themselves. Introduce yourself. Mention the people who recommended them. Ask them whether they handle closings, and whether they have free time now. Then ask whether you can have a consultation with them, without charge; if there's a charge, will it be applied to the total fee?

Other questions to ask a lawyer by phone or, better yet, in person:

☐ Do you specialize in real estate?

☐ How many closings have you handled in the past few years?

☐ What advice can you give a do-it-yourselfer like me?

☐ Are you reachable after hours? Do you have someone covering for you?

☐ Would you qualify potential buyers?

☐ Should I consider giving a buyer a first or second mortgage? If I do, would you draw up the arrangement? Check the buyer's finances and credit rating?

71

- ☐ Will you give me a binder contract to keep in my house?
- ☐ How much earnest money should I demand?
- ☐ Do you have malpractice insurance? (If not, be wary. He may not be able to pay you if you ever win a suit against him.)
- ☐ What are the major services you will perform for me?

Sample Client/Lawyer Agreement*

This agreement is entered into by and between
_____ ("Attorney") and _____ ("Client").

Attorney will perform the following services for Client [here specify the services to be performed]:

_____

_____

_____

Attorney estimates that legal services required by Client will take approximately _____ to _____ hours and cost between _____ and _____ as follows:

_____

_____

[Here the lawyer lists hours and costs for handling different aspects of the case should certain variables occur.]

Disbursement costs [filing fees, deposition and transcript costs, transportation, etc.] will be paid by Client. Attorney estimates that disbursement costs will be as follows:

_____

_____

[Here the lawyer itemizes possible disbursement costs.]

Prior to undertaking work beyond that initially specified Attorney will provide Client with a written estimate of the additional time, fees, and disbursements involved and receive written permission from Client to undertake the work.

Attorney agrees to explain the laws pertinent to Client's problem, the available courses of action, and the attendant risks.

Attorney agrees to notify Client promptly of any

72

☐ Will you yourself handle all the major services— and not, for example, send an apprentice to the closing?

☐ Do you keep duplicates of your records, in case of fire or theft?

☐ How long have you lived in the area? How long have you practiced here?

☐ Do you itemize? Can you send me a sample?

---

significant development and consult with Client in advance on any significant decisions.

Attorney agrees to send Client copy of all pertinent written materials sent or received by Attorney pertaining to Client's case. Client agrees to reimburse Attorney out-of-pocket costs for the reproduction of those materials.

[OR: Attorney agrees to make available to Client for reading in Attorney's office all written materials sent or received by Attorney pertaining to Client's case. At Client's request Attorney will provide copy of any material to Client at Attorney's out-of-pocket costs.]

Attorney agrees to make all reasonable efforts to answer Client's inquiries promptly.

Client agrees to pay Attorney as follows:

_____

_____

_____

[Here describe agreed-upon fee arrangement.]

Client may terminate this agreement, with or without cause, upon written notice to Attorney. Attorney shall return Client's file immediately upon Client's termination of this agreement. Termination shall not affect Client's responsibility to pay for legal services rendered up to the day of termination. Attorney may terminate this agreement for reasons permitted under the _____ [state] Code of Professional Responsibility.

Nothing herein contained shall be interpreted to limit or restrict the Attorney's professional obligations under _____ [state] Bar's codes or canons.

*Source: The National Resource Center for Consumers of Legal Services Inc.

☐ What do you charge to handle a closing? Would it be better for me if you charged by the hour? What about an hourly rate with a maximum?

☐ Would your fee be lower if I employ you when I buy my next house?

☐ Will you charge me if I phone you with a question, or to give you updated information?

☐ Will you give me a contract specifying the employment and fee arrangement? (See the model on the preceding two pages.)

Now that you have become acquainted with your candidates, it's time to choose between them.

In general, look for a lawyer with seven to ten years of experience. And, of course, zero in on a lawyer who specializes in real estate.

A lawyer at a medium-sized firm—four to eight members—may be best. Lawyers who practice independently may not have good backup support, may be more reluctant to consult other legal specialists for advice, and may have a lower standard of ethics (as surveys have indicated). Large law firms, on the other hand, may treat you high-handedly.

Don't hire a lawyer simply because of "good chemistry," as the phrase goes. That can be like marrying purely for love. Good chemistry is certainly desirable, but angelic charm may not protect you against a predaceous buyer and the buyer's manipulative lawyer.

Give the nod to a local lawyer, not one many miles away. The local lawyer is likely to be more familiar with local customs (how escrow money is handled, for example) and to have local connections.

Consider using a lawyer from a clinic: The cost will be low, the quality high. But if anything seems fishy in the arrangement the buyer is proposing, or if you yourself are a mere babe in the woods, you might be safer with an older, more experienced lawyer than the young talents from a legal clinic.

What clients want—and don't want—in lawyers:

Want:	Don't Want:
1. Friendliness	1. Superior attitude
2. Promptness; businesslike manner	2. Bored, indifferent attitude
3. Courtesy	3. Impatience; impersonality; failure to inform
4. Unpretentiousness	
5. Keeping client informed	4. Rudeness; brusqueness

What lawyers want—and don't want—in other lawyers:

Want:	Don't Want:
1. Good results	1. Procrastination
2. Honesty	2. Failure to inform
3. Efficiency	3. Lack of frankness
4. Personality	
5. Education	4. Lack of courtesy

Most of all, lawyers want another lawyer to do a good job, and to be prompt and efficient. The public seems to be unduly taken with a lawyer's personality. This ranking comes from an old study by the Missouri Bar Association.

Once you have narrowed down your list of experienced, trustworthy, competent lawyers, home in on the fee.

Flat fees make it easier to compare what lawyers charge. But you may have to pay incidental costs, such as those for photocopying and for recording documents. And there's also the question: Do you pay extra for phone consultations?

An hourly fee is another possibility, though there's the danger that a not-so-busy lawyer may pad the bill. Check what the hourly fee is for work the lawyer doesn't do—typing by a secretary, for example. You might be able to effect a compromise: an hourly fee, with a preset maximum.

Find out from a banker what the going rate for closings is in your area. As a rough rule, it's 1/2 to 1 percent of the selling price. A few years ago, a survey done by a law firm found that lawyers in California charged $773 on average for handling the closing on a $60,000 house; in the Northeast, $363; in the West, $310; in the South, $307; in the Southwest, $303; in the Midwest, $259.

The average hourly fee for an experienced lawyer in California was $135; in the Midwest, $92; in the South, $95. In the West, apart from California, the fee was $102 an hour; in the Southwest, $114; in the Northeast, $108.

Some good lawyers charge less than some bad lawyers. In hiring a lawyer, you don't necessarily get what you pay for. Still, if one of your candidates is clearly outstanding, be willing to pay a little more for his or her services.

If the main reason you want to sell your house yourself is that you very much need all the money you can get, you might consider one of the more than 1,000 Legal Aid and Legal Services offices in this country. Each has its own standards of eligibility. If you have Social Security disability income or Supplemental Social Security income, you probably qualify.

Once you have hired your lawyer, keep her informed. If you are getting divorced and that might queer the sale of your home, or if your basement leaks a flood, level with your lawyer. Tell her when you haven't taken her advice, too—such as lowering the price of your house.

Read all of the documents sent to you, or at least glance over them.

If you have trouble reaching your lawyer on the phone, try calling at five in the afternoon. You may have less competition.

To learn more about dealing with lawyers, or how to respond when you have a grievance, get in touch with HALT, 1319 F Street, N.W., Suite 300, Washington, D.C. 20004; phone number (202)347-9600. A reformist group, it seems to harbor just the proper amount of skepticism toward the legal profession.

PRETTYING UP THE PLACE

7

A neat price and a neat house—together, they raise your chances of selling your house enormously. Not only that, but a spiffy, well-running, sparklingly decorated house can add thousands to your selling price.

Your first step is to read the riot act to everyone in your family. Finally, at long last, THIS HOUSE MUST BE PRESENTABLE. Explain to one and all that the house must be kept cleaner and neater than ever before. And when a potential buyer is on the way—"Red alert! Red alert!"—every family member must go into his or her act, straightening up assigned areas and rooms.

Why is neatness so important? There are a number of interesting theories.

□ Most buyers cannot tell whether a furnace works properly, whether you have sufficient voltage, if the basement leaks in a heavy rain, or whether termites are tenanting your house. But they *can* recognize cleanliness and neatness, so they pay undue attention. It's comparable to a car buyer who knows nothing whatsoever about cars kicking the tires.

A friend of mine was wavering over buying a rather expensive house. What persuaded him to buy was the inside of a cabinet in the house's basement. Not only were the shelves free of dust, they had been covered with bright lining paper. "If they were *that* meticulous," he says, "how could I go wrong?"

□ Buyers can get distracted when they see a lot of hard work looming on the horizon. In one house I checked out, every single room needed something. Windowpanes were cracked, door hinges had to be oiled, screens were ripped, cracks in walls needed plaster, faucets needed washers, peeling wallpaper had to be glued back, broken molding had to be replaced, a banister was loose, a light switch didn't work. The house itself was an architectural wonder and the price was reasonable, but I just couldn't get as enthusiastic as my wife. I felt like Hercules upon his first sight of the Augean stables.

□ If the owners have neglected minor things, a buyer may figure that they have neglected major things. If the paint on the front door is flaking and the faucets drip, the owners may also have ignored problems with the furnace, the central air, the roof, the boiler, the foundation. The buyer is probably right.

□ A buyer—or a buyer's friend or relative—may be a

snobbish Felix Unger, not appreciative of the Oscar Madison slobbish approach to life. Perhaps, like myself, some buyers can serenely accept a filthy kitchen floor and dishes piled high in the sink when looking at a house. But if a buyer's finicky mother (or father) spots a tiny, almost invisible stain in a dark corner of your carpet, all bets may be off. Felix Ungers do not buy houses from Oscar Madisons. (*The Odd Couple*, in case you forgot.)

Your house is in a sort of beauty contest, and there is only one winner. If the judges—the buyers—must choose between a three-bedroom house with fireplace, den, and carpeting throughout and your house, which is identical except that the front doorbell isn't working, well, try again. In any close race, trivial differences can become important differences.

Preparing your house for sale calls for three steps—or maybe four. First, the casting-out process. Second, cleaning and repairing. Third, prettying up the place. And fourth, possibly having the outside painted.

CASTING OUT

A more spacious house will be easier for you to clean and keep clean. Visitors will also be impressed by the house's roominess.

As a general guide, remove whatever you surely won't be using over the next few years—clothing, furniture, books, records, dishware, souvenirs, the electric fondu pot, old paint cans with paint that might match something but you don't know what, the exercise bicycle that is a permanent indictment of your frail sense of determination.

Be ruthless. If you cannot discard the fondu pot, assign it to the garage sale you'll be holding. Otherwise, store it out of sight—in the attic or basement. Keep in mind that, when you move, as far as transportation charges are concerned, everything you take with you will cost extra.

Start the process by cleaning out the attic and basement, because you can then create room there to store other things you may not be able to part with. Then go through all the other rooms. Naturally, to preserve your marriage and your deteriorating relationship with your children, agree on what gets discarded, what goes into the pile for the garage sale, and what gets stored away.

The golden rule: When in doubt, throw it out.

A garage sale should bring in a little spare money for the prettying-up process. Try to sell some attractive items, to draw in passersby. Ask friends and neighbors to contribute, so you will have an unusually large selection—and you can ask them to spell you.

Label everything with prices, but as the sale draws to a close announce that prices are negotiable.

Tell visitors that your house is going on sale, too, so they can spread the word. Most houses, remember, are sold to nearby residents or to their friends and relatives. Have your fact sheets prominently set out on a table (see the next chapter), and give copies to anyone you talk to who seems interested.

It is a cardinal sin to keep anything remaining after your garage sale. Give the debris away, or throw it out. Yes—old radios, dull, heavy furniture, copies of Reader's Digest Condensed Books. This is the age of obsolescence.

CLEANING UP YOUR ACT

Buy a notebook. Walk through the house, top to bottom, stem to stern, marking down what must be cleaned, what repaired, and who should do it—you, your spouse, your kids, outside help? Leaky faucets, stuck windows, the grimy kitchen ceiling, the moody fluorescent light in the bathroom, the cracked concrete walk outside, the rattly windows, the small, almost invisible stain in one corner of a carpet.

Elbert Hubbard, the American humorist, once said that you can always identify a homeowner. He just emerged from a hardware store.

If you yourself haven't been fixing things regularly, you will have a formidable task in store. Consider calling in help. Find a handyperson through ads in local newspapers or through a local hardware store. Hire a gardener, call in plumbers, painters, electricians, wallpapers, cleaners. People who do heavy-duty housecleaning can take care of floor scrubbing, window washing, furniture polishing, and other awful jobs that the average feather-dusting housecleaner won't.

Okay, now your house is as spiffy as the day you bought it (well, almost). How do you keep it clean and well running? Put throw rugs over well-traveled areas, like the kitchen floor. Consider making certain rooms off limits to the family except in virtual emergencies—the downstairs bathroom, the living room. Set aside an hour on Friday nights—before buyers begin their invasion— to bring everything back to apple-pie order.

Some other tips:

Air the house out periodically, particularly if someone smokes, or if you have pets. As regards animals, your best course is to lend them to a devoted friend for the duration. One real-estate broker has made the out-landish estimate that 50 percent of all buyers don't like animals, are afraid of them, or are allergic. I would estimate 30 percent.

Lighten up the house. Put in brighter bulbs. Open your curtains before buyers arrive. Install new table lamps.

Hide half the children's toys. Store away half of your regular clothes.

Spruce up the furniture, even though you're taking it with you. Nicks, dents, and scratches may irrationally dampen a buyer's enthusiasm.

Pay special attention to the kitchen. It should be spotless, shiny, roomy, and clean—including the ceiling above the oven.

Also pay particular attention to the basement. It's what buyers fear most, and it's the place they tend to visit last, from which they will carry away their final impression of your house.

Basements tend to be dark, smelly, and damp. Make sure yours is well illuminated. Run your dehumidifier for long stretches. Ventilate the place. Scrub and scrub the floor and walls.

A clever way to let sophisticated buyers know that your basement is dry is to put good furniture down there.

Well, is your house a cream puff now? Go visit some other houses for sale—and compare.

PRETTYING UP

The longer you've lived in your house, the more trouble you may have selling it.

Over the years, you may have become accustomed to

84

the old-fashioned kitchen, the faded wallpaper, the ponderous crowd of furniture, the toilet that runs continuously unless you jiggle the handle, the pull-switch light in the closet, the garage door that requires you to turn into the Incredible Hulk to lift it up, the odors from the cats, dogs, hamsters, or whatever else you may have. You probably think everything about your house is *comfortable*. Buyers may think *old*.

Over the years, you may also have gone wild in adapting your house to your own tastes. Studies have shown that buyers are put off by a house that bears the unmistakable imprint of its current owner, whether it's an unusual color scheme, a special room devoted to a collection of stuffed animals, or photographs of your sisters, cousins, and aunts staring down from walls all over the place. I'm proud of the quaint, original covers of old magazines I have on the walls of my own house, from *Ballyhoo* to *The Ladies' Home Companion*. Before I sell, I may replace them with Wyeths. (My wife's taste runs to Brueghel prints; they will have to come down, too.)

Herewith, a true tale of terror, told to me by Harlan Williams, a Realtor in Newark, Delaware:

A family was transferred to Newark by the Ronson Company, which makes lighters. Williams recalls:

> It was a new house they bought. The wife came down here and picked out the colors to go with the house. I don't know where the woman's head was, but she picked out the very darndest things, very vivid lavender and a very vivid kelly green for the dining room, and a mustard yellow for the den. Just about every room you went into was bang, bang, bang, it just hit you. The first thing you saw was the color, not the room.
>
> Well, lo and behold, the fellow was transferred again before they ever moved into the house. The company lived up to its agreement, and took over the house from him and turned it over to us for resale.

Well, we couldn't get people interested in it because of the colors.

The man from Ronson handling the resale would call once in a while, and finally I told him, "You know, you're probably going to smile at this, or get mad, but we're having trouble selling that house because of the colors." And he said, "That's ridiculous." His whole attitude was "You people are not doing your job." So I said, "When are you going to be in Newark?" He said, "I'll be down in a week and a half."

So one morning we went out to look at the house, and he walked into the entrance hall, looked around, peered up the steps, and said, "Paint the son of a bitch."

We had the house sold in about two weeks.

To protect buyers from "territorial anxiety," tone down everything that hints that they are trespassers in your inner sanctum—such as fixtures, furnishings, decorations. If you repaint, use muted colors, like white, off-white, and beige.

The well-to-do are especially prone to self-indulgence. "Because wealthy people can afford to do what they want," says Bruce A. Percelay, president of the Mount Vernon Company in Cambridge, Massachusetts, "they tend to express strong personal tastes in their homes—like very high-style decorating in their wallpaper. Some of them overdo it, and their homes don't appeal to people with more restrained tastes. Bright green carpeting, even at $70 a yard, may diminish a house's appeal."

Don't just tone down your house; gussy it up. Percelay, who, along with Peter Arnold, wrote *Packaging Your House for Profit*, proposes that you begin by asking a few friends and neighbors over for a "focus" session. What do they like about the house? What do they dislike? If they had a thousand dollars to spend on jazzing up the place, what would they do?

A few hundred dollars can go a long way. You can buy

brass wall plates, porcelain handles for cabinets, cut-glass doorknobs, bright shower curtains, snazzy light fixtures, even impressive doorbell chimes. Spend a little more and put a luxurious new screen in front of your fireplace. Or install a telephone in your bathroom (it's easy to remove). Or fill the bathroom with flowering plants.

Your goal: *Every single room in your house should have something special about it that the buyer will be getting with the sale.* That way, when you are escorting prospective buyers through your house, you can boast about these things in every room you visit. The buyers will find the journey more interesting, and more memorable, than similar journeys through other houses.

My own house boasts a recreation-room floor with an imprinted shuffleboard, an electrostatic precipitator for air purity, an intercom system, white textured wallpaper in the living room, shower massagers in the bathrooms, and an avocado-colored refrigerator, dishwasher, and oven in the kitchen.

Percelay, by the way, is a real-estate consultant, and his book is well worth reading. But I found one of his observations somewhat disturbing:

> If a buyer walks into a home and sees the latest colors, he or she will presume that the appliances are new. Conversely, when a buyer walks into a home and sees appliances with discontinued colors like avocado or harvest gold, it suggests the items are dated. But the same set of appliances in white, a color offered all the time, gives no hint of age.

I recently paid *extra* for my avocado-colored appliances.

PAINT THE OUTSIDE?

A house should have "curb appeal," which is why you should consider springing for a paint job before putting your house on the market.

But siding may be the answer if all your house paint would have to be removed first. When painter Donald G. Hogan of Hawthorne, New Jersey, is asked to work on a house that's in dreadful shape because of a previous bad paint job, he says he just walks away. A house covered with paint that's peeling and blistering must have all of it scraped down. "And I've yet to meet a person willing to have all that old paint taken off," he says. "Even on an average-sized house, it can cost $10,000." Siding may cost only $9,000.

The Right Time. Homeowners usually decide to paint simply because their houses seem to need brightening up, says Edwin C. Price of Benjamin Moore & Co. in Montvale, New Jersey, a leading paint manufacturer. "It's like looking at your shoes and deciding that they need a shine."

Usually there's nothing wrong with this attitude. But if yours is a very old house with many coats of paint, the weight of yet another coat may cause cracking. You might be better off not painting, and letting your buyer paint after the weather has had a few years to reduce the paint's thickness.

You virtually *must* paint if the existing coat is deteriorating so that you can see the primer (the paint that helps the regular paint adhere) or the bare wood itself. Consider having only the bad areas repaired. In fact, if only one or two sides show deterioration, you might have them repainted the color of the good sides and leave the good sides alone (nobody may notice that the colors don't quite match). Still, if one area is horrendous, the entire paint job may follow suit shortly.

So, *when* should a house be repainted? The official answer is just before it obviously needs repainting.

Most authorities recommend that a house be painted only when the temperature is between 50 and 90 degrees Fahrenheit. Heat can cause paint to dry too quickly; cold can cause it to clump. Don Hogan, who has painted the houses of former president Richard Nixon and baseball player Tommy John, claims that "The weather actually has more effect on the painter than the paint. On very hot days, or very cold days, he'll do a hasty job—just to get indoors faster."

Early fall is the best time to paint, with early spring next. In the fall the wood will have had all summer to dry out, and there will be fewer bugs around to get caught in the paint.

Tell your painter not to work on a windy day; otherwise, you may get a lot of dirt in your paint. If the weather is threatening, have him return another day (unless latex paint has had a few hours to dry, rain can wash it away).

A good painter will follow the sun. She will start with the sides that have already been exposed to the sun during the day, so the morning dew on the wood will have had a chance to evaporate.

The Right Paint. Although oil-based paints are still popular in New England and there are many old-time painters who swear by them, latex is dominating the field more and more. Latex allows some moisture in the wood to escape. It retains its color better. Unlike the oils, it will swell and shrink with the wood. It doesn't smell so yucky. And you can wash up with water.

But Don Hogan insists that oil-based paints remain the better choice for the trim on a house—the window frames, the shutters, the doors. "I've never seen a latex to match the oil enamel in either hardness or good looks," he says. "And latex enamel doesn't flow out to a fine finish. Latex on trim just doesn't have it." Spokespeople for the latex companies violently disagree.

The paint authorities I spoke with do agree that one coat of paint will do nicely. Use two coats only when you're having trouble covering a dark paint with a lighter paint. "You just don't add that much protection with a second or third coat," says David Sawdey, product and marketing services manager of the consumer paint division of du Pont & Co. in Wilmington, Delaware. "It's not worth it."

But hardly anyone agrees on whether you should ever cover a latex with oil paint, or oil with latex. *Consumer Reports* claims that if you mix breeds, the top layer won't adhere well. Edwin Price of Benjamin Moore scoffs, "There's not one iota of truth in that idea." Hogan suggests a middle course: Never use latex over a shiny oil-based paint. Have the shiny coat sanded down first, so the latex will adhere better.

Don't buy a mess of paint on sale somewhere, then hire a painter and order him to use that paint. The painter may be unfamiliar with its special qualities— and do a bad job. Have the painter use the paint he or she is accustomed to using.

Choosing Colors. If you have your house painted a color that clashes with your neighbors' houses—a pink in an army of whites, say—they may see the hue, and cry. You may also have trouble selling your house. So don't be too unconventional. For something different

90

but not too different, consider those subdued "colonial" colors that are popular now.

In choosing colors, keep in mind that a dark color on a color card will *look darker* on a house, and a light color will *look lighter*. Remember to match the paint on the body of the house with the color of the roof. (You can have the shingles painted if need be.)

To a certain extent, you can use color to change how your house is perceived. A large house will look smaller if it's a dark color. A small house will look larger if it's a light color.

If you have many windows and want to deemphasize them, paint the trim the same color as the frame of the house. You can play down a very tall chimney the same way—paint the mortar the same color as the wood. To make a house look taller, paint the corner boards a different color from the rest of the frame, and in general emphasize vertical lines. You can make a house look longer and lower by painting a horizontal feature a different color—the fasciae, for example. (Fasciae are the boards covering the joints between the tops of the walls and the eaves of the roof.)

These days, many homeowners are using three or even more colors on their houses to emphasize the architectural niceties. Says David Sawdey of du Pont, "If you have attractive architectural details, like turrets and latticework, you may want to accent them by painting them a different color."

Whom to Use. A college kid? An experienced painter? I went the cheap college-kid route a few years ago. To convey what a terrible job he did: I just had my house covered with aluminum siding.

SPREADING THE GOOD WORD

8

Far too many fizzbos buy three to five lines of cheap advertising space in their local shopper, set up a small, hand-painted For Sale sign on their lawns, and are hurt and perplexed by how seldom their phone rings. After a week or two, they give up the good fight and gloomily list their houses with brokers.

Successfully selling your house yourself calls for a full-scale publicity campaign. It can be fun. You get to write! What you write gets published! You can give rein to your imagination! If you normally spend your working days conducting marketing surveys for the newest detergent, here is a perfect opportunity to show the world how creative you really are.

STEP 1. THE FACT SHEET

You may have forgotten a few of the truly desirable, unusual features of your house, so—with fresh eyes—stroll through the inside and outside. On a pad, note anything special: the number of trees in the front and back yards, the underground sprinkler system, the flagstone patio, the circular driveway, the large foyer, the sunken living room, the cathedral ceilings, the exposed beams, the hardwood or parquet floors, the wall-to-wall carpeting, the stone fireplace, the built-in bookshelves, the kitchen with a dining nook, the spiral staircase, the dressing area and the twin sinks in the bathroom, the finished basement, the heated garage, and so forth.

Just for fun, here are a few amenities mentioned in actual advertisements for ritzy houses, those selling typically for $600,000 and up:

- □ "Approximately 415 acres with 3,675 feet of beachfront on the Atlantic Ocean" (in the Bahamas)
- □ "Even the garage has oak floors and imported tile flooring"
- □ "Fireplace a replica of one in the American Wing of the Metropolitan Museum of Art"
- □ "200 can be served at indoor buffet luncheons and suppers"
- □ "Recently Paul Newman and Joanne Woodward used it as a location for a movie"
- □ "A regulation indoor bowling alley'
- □ "Three stairways to the first floor"
- □ "Handmade sterling silver shell-shaped sink"

- "Mink and antique Tibetan rugs"
- "Over 100 paintings, including a Picasso and a Miro"
- "A fireman's pole from the kitchen to the children's bedroom above"
- "Soda fountain with sink"
- "The 45 sumptuous rooms include seven bedrooms plus servants', 17 bathrooms, and 15 fireplaces of marble and wood"
- "Color TV in all 10 bedrooms"
- "Sixty-one solid-core doors are individually hand-crafted"
- "There is an air-conditioned doghouse"
- "Seven-car garage with two apartments"
- "8,000-foot miniature railroad, 40-passenger capacity"
- "Chapel: 10 pews, with stained-glass windows"
- "Its own 53-acre lake"
- "Heliport adjacent to the croquet field"

If your own house isn't quite as conspicuously consumptive as these, don't despair. Even a built-in dishwasher, stainless steel sinks, colored bathroom fixtures, a formal dining room instead of a "great room" (combined living room and dining room), and a one-car attached garage can be selling points.

Now that you have reacquainted yourself with the virtues of your house and grounds, get to work on your fact sheet. It's usually a single page, sometimes with a photograph or drawing.

Begin by assembling the basic data: where your house is, whether it's brick, frame, stone, stucco, or shingle, the size of the property, the house's age, the cost of heating, electricity, and taxes, and so forth.

On the facing page is a form you can improvise upon.

As the headline, you might use the style of the house ("All-Brick Colonial") or the area ("Greenwich, Connecticut") rather than "For Sale by Owner." (Buyers prefer brick to frame. But just as men supposedly prefer blondes and marry brunettes, most buyers wind up with frame houses. They're cheaper.)

Change the order of the items, if you wish, to dramatize the house's strong points (its age, if new, for example). Give yourself extra space to expand on any feature—if you have, say, a bathroom with a sauna, marble sinks, safety features like railings, a dressing area, a linen closet, and tiled floors and walls.

Mention luxuries not indicated on the fact sheet shown here: pools, balconies, decks, water softeners, a slate roof, a burglar-alarm system, a built-in humidifier. List the brand names of appliances if they're well known.

At the bottom, unleash your creativity. Provide a succinct but vivid description of your property, such as "A modern house with many of the latest luxuries—from built-in microwave oven and garbage disposal to a sauna and entertainment room. Spacious and sunny inside; spacious and shady outside. Spotless—and easy to maintain. We've loved living here."

This particular fact sheet stresses the factual rather than the flowery. Another approach—simpler, more colorful—is the one Charles and Diane Thompson created with a computer, on light-blue paper (see pp. 204–205). But the italic type and capital letters may be a little difficult to read.

Once you have polished off your masterpiece, have a local printer run off at least 100 copies.

FOR SALE BY OWNER

Price:_____ Style:_____
Owners: _____
Address: _____
Phone numbers: _____
Directions: _____
Room sizes:
  Living room—   Kitchen—
  Dining room—   Family room—
  Master bedroom—   Other bedrooms—

Bathrooms: _____
Garage: _____
Fireplace: _____
Patio: _____
Porch: _____
Closets: _____
Basement: _____
Heating: _____
Air conditioning: _____
Insulation: _____
Appliances: _____
Size of lot: _____
Age of house: _____
Personal property included: _____
Local schools: _____
Houses of worship: _____
Transportation: _____
Taxes: _____
Heating/cooling costs: _____
Possible financing: _____
Summary: _____

STEP 2. THE GRAPEVINE

Perhaps one out of five houses is sold by word of mouth. A Rotary Club member may mention at a luncheon, "My brother-in-law is thinking of moving around here, so we'll have another Rotarian." Someone responds, "Is he looking for a house? One around the corner is going on sale."

Begin your word-of-mouth campaign by phoning the personnel departments of local hospitals, colleges, large businesses, law firms. Ask the people there if they know of any transferees who will be looking for houses in your vicinity, and, if so, may you mail them your fact sheet? Do likewise with ministers, priests, and rabbis. (Smart buyers, before moving to a new area, check with the local clergy; they obtain truthful, accurate assessments of the best schools and the best sections of town.) Ask the clergy whether you can put up a photo of your house and a fact sheet in their church. Also consider posting notices in other community facilities, like a country club or even a supermarket.

Pass the word to your friends that your house is for sale, and ask for advice. Where should you advertise? What should you emphasize about your home? Would they drop by sometime and suggest changes you might make? Would they post one of your fact sheets at their place of business?

You might also emulate real-estate agents and send postal cards to everyone within a few blocks to announce that your house is for sale. Neighbors often have friends or relatives eager to move nearby.

As mentioned, if you hold a garage sale (or tag sale, porch sale, or whatever it's called), have your fact sheets available.

STEP 3. THE "FOR SALE" SIGN

The sign reflects the house. It should suggest high quality, neatness, care, and concern. It must not look cheap and jerry-built.

The usual recommendations are dark letters, 21 inches high by 28 inches wide, on a white background, which is easily readable by drivers going in either direction past your house. It should say:

FOR SALE

444-3583

Call for appointment.

STEP 4. ADVERTISING

Keep track of how much you spend on ads, trying to stay within a budget of 1/2 to 1 percent of your offering price ($400 to $800 for an $80,000 house).

In general, avoid the small local papers and concentrate on the large dailies, the ones with plenty of real-estate advertising. Advertise on Saturdays and Sundays; covering both days may entitle you to a discount.

Use larger ads for expensive houses. If you buy a five-line ad for a $350,000 house, suitable buyers may just skip past—and, in any case, you may not have the space to let readers know that the asking price is justified. If yours is an inexpensive, garden-variety house, keep your ads small, so as not to stretch your budget.

Vary the ads you run; have two or three versions. One might be short and fact filled; another might be longer, and feature a little purple prose ("immaculate," "luxurious," "elegant," "secluded," "lovely," "breathtaking," "spectacular"). A third ad might be a compromise—factual and, if not purple, at least with a tinge of violet. Personally, I prefer "beautiful large yard" to "lrg yrd," "enormous stone fireplace" to "frplc," and "spacious sunny kitchen with dining nook" to "EIK."

If you run the same ad week after week, buyers will become familiar with it, and perhaps conclude, simply because your house is not selling quickly, that something is wrong. Also, by varying the appeal of your ads, you may attract both the spouse who wants the prosaic as well as the spouse seeking the poetic. One might phone.

Plan to blitz the papers with ads in the spring, when buyers begin sprouting. In winter, when buyers are as scarce as 70-degree days, be more restrained, with respect to both size and frequency.

Try as much as you possibly can to avd bflg abbns.

The first ad you run might say, JUST ADVERTISED. That should grab the attention of buyers who have been scouting the area for a while, who know there's always a chance that a house freshly on the market may be a cream puff, a bargain, or both. Other ads you run might carry the headline, FOR SALE BY OWNER, or something flowery, like GRACIOUS & CAPACIOUS.

Start your text with the location. Most buyers know which areas they want to live in, and will be looking for "Greenwich," "Ridgewood," "Westport," or "Beverly Hills." If yours is a specially desirable area of town, mention that, too: "Passaic Park," not just "Passaic."

Give the price, without prefacing it with "asking." Say "firm" if you mean it and if your house is very reasonably priced.

Include the style of the house and the number of bedrooms and bathrooms. In mentioning the kitchen, living room, and dining room, try to add impressive details. Then proceed to special features, like a fireplace, den, finished basement, attached two-car garage, and so forth. (To refresh your memory, refer to your fact sheet.) I myself find "Many extras" intriguing.

Once you have written your ad, compare it with the ads in last week's newspaper. Are they more colorful, more detailed? Is yours rather leaden and dull by comparison? If so, it's back to your typewriter.

Here are some actual ads from a recent issue of my local newspaper:

CLOSTER. $225,000
Completely remodeled, 2 BRs, 1 1/2 bth Col. Lrg LR
w/frplc, very new kit, den, 2 car gar, deck, in a great
loc. By owner, princ only, 756-9864

Comment: Seems rather high-priced for a two-bedroom home. I would like to know a little more. The house seems undistinguished. Is there a large yard? Is the kitchen big enough for a dining nook? What's "great" about the location?

FAIR LAWN-Tudor Col. 4BR, 2 bth, famrm, 2 car
gar, great loc, walking distance to NY transp, house of
worship Asking $230,000. By owner. 529-7356.

Comment: In this instance, I would rather know more about the house than about its location. No fireplace? Nothing special about the kitchen? ("Mod kit" would help.) Again, the house seems undistinguished.

HAWTHORNE-For sale by owner.
Charming, roughgarden, 3BR Col. EIK, FDR, lrg LR
w/frplc, att gar, many extras. Easy commute to NYC.
Fenced yd, perfect for children. $219,000. 842-3017.

Comment: Many buyers might call just to inquire what a "roughgarden" is. (The name of the architect.) The details here make the ad stand out—"charming," the name of the respected architect, the "formal dining room" (FDR), the attached garage, the fenced yard. Why is this ad so much better than the other two? One reason is that it has an extra line of text.

MAHWAH CRAGMERE PARK
Charming fieldstone Colonial nestled on 175 ft. deep
prop. w/brick walkways & patio. Mod. int. blends
w/Old World Charm of fieldstone frplc. Kitch w/
ceramic tile, 3BRs + 2nd flr solarium. Beautifully
maintained & appealing. By Owner, $229,500. Call
348-0032 or 453-5430.

Comment: This is just about the same price house as
in the first ad, yet it's ever more distinctive. ("Mod.
int."—for "Modern interior"—might give someone
pause, though.) It's nine lines—and the four extra lines
will undoubtedly pull in many more phone calls than
the first two ads.

PARK RIDGE $274,000
TWO FAMILY DUPLEX
Situated in park-like setting, this lovely duplex features 5 rms per side, spacious property, wooded sur-
roundings & a quiet dead-end loc. Completely remodeled w/new kit, W/W crptg, lg deck, frplc & much
more. Incls 2 car attached gar, separate laundry rm,
workshop and bsmt. All utils are separate. FOR SALE
BY OWNER Call Eves/Wknds 864-4390

Comment: A bit wordy, but the ad does paint a rustic
picture and provides essential information.

PARADISE VALLEY, ARIZONA
A mansion on a mountain, this 36-room house stands
on an equal number of acres atop Sugarloaf Mountain,
with 360-degree views of the desert and valleys. With
14 bedrooms and 15 baths, the 31,000-square-foot
house glories in such luxuries as inlaid walnut walls
and doors, terrazzo flooring, and eight marble fireplaces imported from Portugal and Italy. There are
decks on all three levels, and its spaces include a study
and a library, as well as a formal dining room. To
delight the winter sports lover, there's an indoor ice-
skating rink. There is also an Olympic-sized swimming pool . . .

Comment: No, this ad did not appear in my local newspaper, but in a special magazine published by a company, Previews, specializing in unusual residences. The house—several years ago—was on the market for $11 million.

The next chapter will focus on how to cope with the flood of phone calls that your fact sheet, your word-of-mouth campaign, your For Sale sign, and your ads have elicited.

SELLING WITHOUT MANIPULATING

In trying to "close" a buyer (persuade the buyer to make an offer), one real-estate agent carries the contract in his hand while escorting the prospect through a house. Supposedly the buyer then becomes accustomed to seeing the document, and doesn't faint dead away when the agent whips it out of his briefcase.

After the tour, the agent leads the buyer to a comfortable, homey area (usually the kitchen) and sits her down. He then takes out a pen, and— apparently by accident—drops it on the floor. He searches in the wrong place: "Where *did* that pen go?" Courteously the buyer retrieves the pen and offers it to the agent. The agent ignores it. But now, with the contract out in the open and the pen in the buyer's hand, the agent gently suggests that the buyer begin filling in the blank spaces . . . .

That is typical of the manipulative way to sell a house. But to be a successful fizzbo, you need not sink so low.

At this point, though, you will be dealing with buyers directly.

Try to be calm, not anxious. Laid back and confident, not aggressive. Remind yourself that there are a great many potential customers out there, and you need only one. You yourself bought the house once upon a time; soon you will encounter someone else with your own refinement and taste.

And never be anything less than graceful under pressure—even if a buyer smirkingly remarks that your avocado-colored kitchen appliances belong in a museum.

HANDLING PHONE CALLS

Place a fact sheet next to every phone in your house. When buyers call, you can rattle off the directions and quickly answer more questions they ask . . .

"I'm calling about the house for sale?"

"Yes, hi there. My name's Mary Mallon. What's yours?"

"George Soper."

"Are you looking for a home in this area? A Colonial?"

"Yes, I think so. Your ad didn't mention the size of the property . . . "

"It's a full acre. The ad also didn't mention a lot of other extras the house has—like built-in bookcases, walk-in closets, central vacuum .... You're not a real-estate agent, are you?"

"No . . . and my other habits are good."

"Where do you live, Mr. Soper? Do you have a house now?"

"We live in Manhattan. We're selling our co-op, and we're looking for a house in the suburbs."

"Can I answer any questions you have about my place?"

"Well, what school district are you in?"

"The Byrd school."

"Good, that's the one I wanted."

"When would you like to stop by? How about tonight at 7 o'clock?"

"Okay. What's your address?"

"It's 150 River Street. What's your phone number, by the way? In case something comes up and I'm not home—or somebody puts a binder on the house before you arrive."

"444-3583. And I know where River Street is—I can find it."

"Is that home or office?"

"My home. My office number is 368-4242."

"Where do you work? In the city?"

"Yes, for P&G."

"Okay, I've scheduled some other people . . . "

In this interview, you have learned the name of the buyer, his phone numbers, and where he works. (If you're at all suspicious, you can check up on him. Just phone before he's supposed to arrive to remind him of the appointment, and confirm that he works at P&G.) You have also begun "qualifying" him (making sure he can afford your house by learning that he already owns a co-op). And you have been ready to filter him out, in case the house really isn't what he wants, by answering his questions (about the school district).

What if you are a woman alone in your house one morning, and a buyer calls?

"Hi, my name's George Soper, and you have a house for sale?"

"Yes, my name's Mary Mallon. Are you looking for a Colonial in this area?"

"Yes, but I'm from the West Coast, and I have to fly back tonight. Can I come over right now? Your house sounds *perfect* for my wife and me. What's your address?" (Obviously, this is suspicious.)

"Well, I don't want to waste your time if this house isn't really what you're looking for. Are you sure you can afford the price? Are you a homeowner now? Where do you work?"

Or: "I have someone coming in a few minutes. Why don't you give me your phone number, and I'll call you back when the coast is clear?" (If he replies, "I'm at a phone booth nearby," forget it.) If you do let him come over, you can conspire with a neighbor to watch when the buyer drives up, and phone you a few minutes after you and the buyer have entered your house.

Once, when I visited a house being sold by a woman who was alone, I learned that she had arranged to telephone a neighbor at a precise time, to report that everything was okay.

But perhaps the best course with someone from out of town who must come over right away—or with someone who asks, despite the "By Appointment" on your For Sale sign, to see the house this minute—is a firm no. Tell him that he can visit only in the evening, when your husband the policeman will be home.

Some other tips:

☐ Schedule visits 45 minutes apart. Usually a tour takes a half-hour.

☐ If no one is at home during the day, buy a phone-answering machine.

☐ Hide valuables before anyone comes, or put them in a safe-deposit box.

☐ If you haven't exiled your pets, keep them outside or in a spare room when visitors come.

☐ Keep a log of your visitors and their phone numbers. You might phone them later for their comments. They may be more frank over the phone, giving you useful suggestions ("The wallpaper in the kitchen is a fright," or "The price seems out of line for a house in that area"), or even reassurance ("I loved the house, but our grand piano wouldn't fit into the living room," or "We're really not ready to buy—we just wanted to see what comparable houses are selling for").

THE GRAND TOUR

Manipulative real-estate agents, in driving buyers to a house, take the most scenic route, bypassing the nearby bowling alley or train station.

If the house is dreary from the outside, they tool right up into the driveway and quickly escort buyers inside.

They warn the buyers that someone else is about to put a binder on the house, and is only waiting (say) for his wife (or her husband) to see it tomorrow. (One lawyer, Benny Kass of Washington, D.C., claims that if you believe real-estate agents, "The entire Red Chinese Army is ready to buy that home you're looking at.") This can be a powerful tactic if a buyer is somewhat interested. Not only is there competition, but someone else apparently thinks the house is desirable. I once fell for this tactic myself. There supposedly was another buyer, ready to put a deposit on the house as soon as his uncle the plumber inspected the place. That night it finally dawned on me (I was young) that there *was* no other buyer, and—amazingly—the house lost much of its appeal.

If there is an obvious flaw in a house, agents have ready answers. Either they pooh-pooh the flaw, or they distract the buyer. The following are actual examples in a book for real-estate agents:

"There's no dining room."
"One less room to clean."

"My, what a dirty house!"
"Yes, but look at the price."

Agents are also *enthusiastic!* "Look at those large bedrooms! . . . It's not often you see real hardwood floors like this . . . . Gosh, they must have paid extra for those avocado-colored appliances!" Enthusiasm is contagious!

They escort buyers rapidly through small, dismal rooms, lingering in the large, bright, well-furnished ones.

Asked questions, agents may not reply until they know what the correct answers are:

"Are there many children in the neighborhood?"
"Do you like a neighborhood with children?"

"No, we like peace and quiet."
"Hardly a brat around for blocks."

If a house is your basic box and has no dining room, and the yard is filled with garbage, an agent might spin romantic dreams, gushing about replacing the windows with French doors and creating an outdoor dining court, complete with sparkling fountain.

Or an agent can say, "Can't you just see yourselves sitting in your cozy living room with the fireplace crackling? Junior is playing downstairs in the rec room with his playmates now, but in a few minutes all of them will go out to play in the backyard, which is completely fenced. You have installed a swing set underneath the big oak tree in the rear of the shaded lot. You look out your window and you see the quiet suburban solitude which makes you feel restful and at peace with the world. The whole house is cozy because of the storm windows and you are able to relax knowing that the payments are within reach. Each month you are building equity and forming a strong, stable family life . . . . You relax in the knowledge that as your son graduates from college your house will be paid for and worth a good deal more than what you have paid . . . ." (No, this isn't satire. It comes from a 1967 book written by a broker for other agents.)

Agents go on and on, in books and articles they write, about the proper words to use (when people study a simple subject too intently, they tend to lose their sanity): "Agreement," not "contract," which suggests constraint. Not "down payment," but "initial investment." The first supposedly summons up thoughts of many payments to come; the second, a shrewd deal. No, not "deal," but "transaction," which is classier. Not "Would you like to buy this home?" but "Would you like to invest in this home?" And, lest the buyer be intimidated by the enormous prices, agents may leave off the "thousands" when mentioning numbers: "The house is going for 80," not "80,000."

To close buyers, agents may set a trap. The buyer says, "The living room is too dark." Replies the agent, "Would you want the owner to paint the living room? Then let's write it into the contract." (*Takes out contract.*)

Agents may also try conditioning buyers into answering yes:

"It's a nice area, isn't it?"
"Yes."
"You wanted a house with four bedrooms, didn't you?"
"Yes."
"Shall we offer to buy the house for a thousand less, to cover repainting the living room?"

Fizzbos can certainly learn a few things from experienced agents, though. Among them:

□ Don't talk too much. Give buyers a chance to think, to admire, to whisper among themselves. Too much talking on your part can be distracting; it can suggest that you're overly anxious to sell.

□ When you take buyers through your house, create interest and diversion by *doing* things. Open closet doors, run water in sinks, turn on the oven, open the refrigerator door, switch on the chandelier.

□ Ask the buyers questions; their answers can guide you toward selling points you should stress. Do they have children? How many, and what ages? ("This is the best school district in town, and there's a playground within walking distance.") Do they like gardening? ("I grow all sorts of vegetables outside—fresh vegetables are so much better.") Do they like woodworking? ("I have a terrific workshop downstairs.")

□ Don't point out the obvious—the wall-to-wall carpeting, for instance. But draw attention to something special: "The view from here is wonderful—you can see the lake down there. Come look." And mention whatever buyers might not notice, such as the triple-pane window glass or the three-zoned heating.

□ If the buyers object to anything, you can just shrug it off and talk about something else. Or you can gently try to persuade them that you haven't found any problem: "The closet in here is small." "Yes, but it's the child's room, and she doesn't need a big closet." Or: "Yes, but we have an enormous storage area in the attic."

□ Remember not to deceive the buyer (see Chapter 5). "Is the basement dry?" "In heavy rains, it gets damp. We run a dehumidifier there occasionally. But we've had no real floods."

□ Give every buyer who drops in a fact sheet.

□ Save time by allowing the tour to end quickly. "Would you like to see the attic? The basement?" If the answer is "No, thanks," the buyers are probably not interested. But they may be back, so remain affable.

□ If they drop hints that they are interested—they seem reluctant to leave, or they ask to see certain rooms again—offer them coffee or tea. You might then give them an opportunity to talk together: "I left something upstairs—I'll be back in a few minutes." Or be open: "Shall I let you two talk together? I can return in a few minutes."

113

□ To prod bashful buyers a bit, you might say, "I have another couple coming in fifteen minutes. Do you want to put a binder on the house? I have contracts here. Do you have a lawyer?"

Of course, if you insist, you could take out a pen, drop it, and pretend you can't find it . . . .

QUALIFYING BUYERS

Real-estate people warn fizzbos about the intimidating task of "qualifying" buyers—the superhuman tact needed to elicit personal financial information from them, the advanced math required to calculate whether they can actually afford your house.

Well, a best-selling book for real-estate agents forthrightly states, "Agents often skip the qualifying interview when working with buyers for the first time."

But agents certainly should qualify buyers, and so should you. Otherwise, later on you may be thrown into a dither because the buyers failed to

10

obtain a mortgage or scrape up the down payment—and your house may not be sold, even though you received a binder contract.

If the idea of qualifying buyers repels you, you can turn the job over to your lawyer, or refer the buyer to local lenders and wait to hear their reports. But that will take time.

True, many successful fizzbos do little or nothing in this regard. A seemingly prosperous couple arrives; they are selling their own high-priced house; both are employed; they are not fazed by your offering price. They may already have a lender's approval for a mortgage, and don't need your help or guidance.

Under such circumstances, you can just go through the motions of qualifying them—unless a check of theirs bounces, or a routine phone call to their offices reveals that they no longer work there, or they refuse to sign your Buyer Qualification Sheet, which states that they have had no credit problems for the past ten years. Getting prospects to sign is important. Up to 1987, only 10 percent of mortgage lenders had been informing credit agencies when their clients defaulted. Now mortgage lenders must report defaults. Still, the person who wants to buy your house this year or next could have lost a few houses along the way by foreclosure, and that might not even appear in his official credit history.

The buyers who should really put the fear of God into you are young people looking for their first home, filled with radiant optimism, counting on raises in their jobs and gifts from relatives, meanwhile wondrously ignorant of heating and air-conditioning costs, the price of lawn mowers, the need for new furniture that fits particular rooms, the fees charged by plumbers and electricians these days. (Actually, their fees may always have

CONFIDENTIAL
Buyer Qualification Sheet

Names: _____Ages: _____
Address: _____
Dependents: _____Ages: _____
Phone numbers: Office _____Home _____
Preferred down payment: _____Maximum: _____
Preferred monthly payment: _____Maximum: _____

	Husband	Wife
Employer:	_____	_____
Address:	_____	_____
Title:	_____	_____
Years:	_____	_____

Family earnings:

19	$	19	$	19	$

	Monthly	Yearly
Husband's income:	$_____	$_____
Other income:	_____	_____
Wife's income:	_____	_____
Other income:	_____	_____
Debts: (subtract)	(_____)	(_____)
TOTAL	_____	_____

TAXES (federal, state, local) you expect to pay this year:

Assets	Debts		
		Monthly Payment	Balance
Cash: _____	Auto:	_____	_____
Stocks, bonds, etc.: _____	Real estate:	_____	_____
Real estate: _____	Loans:	_____	_____
Other: _____	Other:	_____	_____

Have you had any serious credit problems in the past ten years, like a mortgage foreclosure, bankruptcy, receivership, or wage garnishment?

Yes ____ No ____

Date: _____ Signatures: _____

_____

been high. Mark Twain once said that he visited Europe on $500 that his plumber didn't know he had.)

People do get turned down when they apply for mortgages—especially young, overly optimistic buyers.

WHEN TO QUALIFY BUYERS

It's usually time to ask buyers financial questions when they show a serious interest in your home, such as by inquiring whether the appliances go with the house, or whether you will come down a bit on the price.

Qualifying buyers before bargaining with them serves a few purposes besides just making sure they can afford your price.

It can accustom them to the sobering thought of actually buying a house.

It can also guide you with regard to price negotiations. You may be more willing to lower your price if the buyers seem ideal: They can afford a huge down payment and have preliminary approval on a mortgage. If they have already begun selling their own home, you may have no trouble scheduling convenient closing and move-in dates. But if the buyers have not even advertised their home for sale yet, or they rent and are vague about a down payment, or they begin slyly hinting that they expect you to "take back some paper" (provide a first or second mortgage), they are not quite ideal, and there may be no reason to encourage them with price concessions.

HOW TO QUALIFY BUYERS

To be thorough, ask your local banker or mortgage company (1) the maximum mortgage it would lend on your house (if you had your house formally appraised, the bank or mortgage company should tell you); (2) what down payment it would expect (usually 20 percent of the selling price); (3) what gross annual income the buyers need to afford your selling price; and (4) what other key questions you should ask the buyers.

Now, let's suppose that a buyer has said, "Would you take $83,000 for the place?" You might reply, "Well, it's awfully low, but maybe we can work something out . . . . You wouldn't be offended if I asked you some questions about your finances, would you? . . . I apologize for asking them, but in order to sell my house without an agent, and keep the price low, I have to do some of the work that an agent normally does . . . . Would you mind helping me fill out this form? [Yes, the one on page 117.] It should take only a few minutes, and you can use estimates. I couldn't answer some of these questions myself, off the top of my head!"

You might lead the buyers into a secluded area, so that details about their finances aren't overheard by other buyers who may be waiting around.

Ask some nonthreatening questions to begin with. "Where do you live now? Do you own a house? Are you selling it?"

You need not go through the entire Buyer Qualification Sheet if the buyers inspire confidence, or if you think you might have been a little too eager to qualify them (they're looking unhappy). You can skip the section on assets and debts, for example. But pay attention to the down payment they can afford, and their total yearly income.

THE QUICK AND DIRTY APPROACH

Here is a rough guide as to whether the buyers can afford your home: The selling price is no more than two to two and a half times their (combined, if applicable) gross annual income minus their long-term debts—for car payments, for alimony or child support, for educational loans, and so forth.

If you're selling your house for $90,000, the buyers need a total gross annual income of $45,000—or, at the very least, $36,000. And $36,000 is dubious.

If their income is only $36,000 or less, don't be too quick to discourage them. If they can afford a large down payment—25 percent or more—they may be able to swing it. Perhaps they are profiting from the sale of their own home, or are relying on gifts from relatives. A large down payment will reduce their mortgage payments directly and perhaps indirectly: In return, lenders may lower their interest rates.

If the buyers don't pass the two to two and a half times test, matters look bleak. I once did an informal survey and found that people typically get into hot water, financially, when they (1) lose their jobs or (2) make a down payment on a house. The down payment strips them of emergency funds—for unexpected medical expenses not covered by insurance, for replacing cars needed for jobs, for legal problems, for tax problems. If the buyers make an unusually large down payment to reduce their mortgage expenses, they may become vulnerable to myriad economic reverses—and your sale may fall through.

Perhaps you should tactfully suggest that they return when they have preliminary approval on a mortgage.

THE OFFICIAL APPROACH

In the view of many lenders, shelter expenses should not exceed 33 percent of an applicant's gross monthly income.

Let's say that the buyers have a gross monthly income of $3,000 ($36,000 a year), and they want a $90,000 house. For the mortgage they are seeking, they would pay $800 a month. For real-estate taxes, 1.5 percent of the house price ($112.50). For insurance, .5 percent ($37.50). For operating expenses, 3 percent ($225). For repairs, 1 percent ($75).

Add up the costs: $800 + $112.50 + $37.50 + $225 + $75 = $1,250. Divide $1,250 by their monthly income ($3,000), and you get 41.6 percent. They will be extraordinarily lucky to get a mortgage.

To try to qualify a buyer using this method, turn to the mortgage table given on page 123.

THE ELABORATE APPROACH

If there's a serious question whether the buyers can afford your house, and you don't want to send them away to search for a mortgage, try qualifying them in more depth.

In general, *a family can afford 40 percent of its spendable income for housing.*

You can use the figures from the Buyer Qualification Sheet to do the sample calculations below.

Husband's yearly income	$ _____	$24,000
Wife's yearly income	$ _____	$12,000
Gross income	$ _____	$36,000
Income taxes (subtract)	($ _____)	($ 6,500)
After-tax income	$ _____	$29,500
Annual debt repayments (subtract)	($ _____)	($ 2,000)
Spendable income	$ _____	$27,500
40% available for housing	$ _____	$11,000
Housing expenses* (subtract)	($ _____)	($ 4,400)
Available for mortgage	$ _____	$ 6,600

*Calculate your own yearly expenditures for real-estate taxes, utilities, insurance, maintenance, and so forth—everything except mortgage payments.

Let's assume that the buyers want a 30-year fixed-rate mortgage (to keep their payments low), and might get one at 10 percent. From the table on the next page, you can figure out that $6,600 will pay for a $62,642 mortgage. If they can manage a 20 percent down payment, divide the $62,642 by 80 percent to find the house they can afford: $78,302. If they can manage a 25 percent down payment, they can spring for an $83,523 house.

Your offering price, remember, is $90,000. Even with a 25 percent down payment, these buyers seem a little out of their league.

Again, your best course may be to send the buyers out to seek financing on their own.

Meanwhile, keep showing your house.

HOW BIG A MORTGAGE CAN THE BUYERS AFFORD?

This table lists the yearly payments required for each $1,000 of a fixed-rate mortgage.

Use the mortgage's interest rate and term to find the yearly cost. Divide the yearly cost into the amount of money the buyers have available every year for a mortgage. Multiply the result by $1,000 to get the maximum mortgage they can afford.

Example: The buyers have $10,000 a year available for

Interest Rate (%)	Length of Mortgage			
	15 years	20 years	25 years	30 years
8	$114.72	$100.44	$92.64	$88.08
8¼	116.52	102.36	94.68	90.24
8½	118.20	104.16	96.72	92.28
8¾	120.00	106.08	98.76	94.44
9	121.88	108.00	100.80	96.60
9¼	123.60	109.92	102.84	98.76
9½	125.40	111.96	104.88	100.92
9¾	127.20	113.88	107.04	103.20
10	128.95	115.80	109.08	105.36
10¼	130.79	117.84	111.12	107.52
10½	132.65	119.76	113.28	109.80
10¾	134.51	121.80	115.44	111.96
11	136.39	123.84	117.60	114.24
11¼	138.28	125.88	119.76	116.52
11½	140.18	127.92	121.92	118.80
11¾	142.10	130.80	124.20	121.08
12	144.02	132.12	126.36	123.48
12¼	145.96	134.23	128.61	125.75
12½	147.90	136.34	130.84	128.07
12¾	149.86	138.46	133.90	130.40
13	151.83	140.59	135.34	132.74
13¼	153.81	142.73	137.60	135.09
13½	155.80	144.88	139.88	137.45
13¾	157.80	147.05	142.16	139.81
14	159.81	149.22	144.45	142.18
14¼	161.82	151.41	146.75	144.56
14½	163.90	153.60	149.06	146.95
14¾	165.90	155.80	151.38	149.34
15	167.95	158.01	153.70	151.73
15¼	170.01	160.24	156.03	154.14
15½	172.08	162.47	158.37	156.54
15¾	174.16	164.70	160.71	158.95
16	176.24	166.95	163.07	161.37

mortgage payments. They can obtain an 11 percent mortgage for 25 years. Their yearly payment, listed below, is $117.60 per $1,000. Divide $117.60 into the $10,000 available, to get 85.034. Multiply by $1,000 to get $85,034—the mortgage they can afford.

The maximum mortgage buyers usually can obtain is 80 percent of the price of the house. So divide $85,034 by 80 percent. The result—$106,292.51—is the price of the house they can afford.

HAGGLING OVER THE PRICE

11

SCENARIOS

Your selling price is $115,000, but you would be agreeable to driving off with $110,000, and you might grumpily settle for $105,000 if the other terms were enticing—you don't have to help the buyer with financing, you can move out quickly, and so forth.

What would you do if . . .

☐ The buyer says, "The Renoir over the fireplace, the William Morris furniture, the Bosendorfer piano, the Tiffany lamps, the Rothschild wines, and the Mercedes-Benz in the driveway come with the house, of course."

Answer: If someone asks for champagne, he or she may be hoping for Perrier instead of tap water. Your task is to make the tap water sound good. "Well, no," you might respond. "But the light fixtures will stay, and the carpeting. And I'm thinking of offering you the fireplace equipment, the washer and dryer, and the avocado-colored refrigerator and dishwasher at bargain-basement prices." (The buyer is entitled to whatever is attached to the house, like light fixtures, although you could substitute comparable ones. Who is entitled to the fireplace equipment is anyone's guess.)

◻ The buyer says, "Why are you moving? Buy another house? Lose your job? Divorce?"

Answer: If you're under pressure to sell quickly, never let the buyer—or even your broker, if you ever hire one—suspect. The buyer will figure that you're under the gun and be unyielding in his negotiations.

"The house is too big, too roomy," you might say. Or, "We want to move closer to our parents." Or, "We've been wondering why ourselves. Why are we leaving those gracious neighbors? The low taxes? The superb school system, the courteous cops, the affable firefighters . . . the precious memories? Maybe we'll take the house off the market."

◻ Says the buyer, "Your roof looks old, your furnace is rusty and makes godawful noises, the suede wallpaper is weird, the furniture looks as though it came from the Salvation Army, and that dog of yours is the most disgusting-looking animal I've ever seen. I wouldn't give you $100,000 for the house."

Answer: Say, "Make it $115,000, and when I leave, I'll take the Salvation Army furniture and that disgusting-looking dog with me."

Control your temper even if buyers are tactless enough to denigrate your house and your taste. And don't let their criticism rattle your confidence that yours is a splendid house at a reasonable price. Remind buyers (and yourself) of the house's good points—the four bedrooms, the central air conditioning, whatever. Suggest that the buyers hire a house engineer to inspect the roof and the furnace, and mention that replacing wallpaper costs only a few hundred dollars.

Someone who sneers at your house and your taste is not only rude, but is probably preparing to make a serious offer. If the churl winds up offering you $115,000, though, I wouldn't blame you for selling your house to someone else for a little less.

□ The young couple are cheery and charming; they're so all-American they might work at Disneyland. They drove up in a banged-up old pickup truck, and they're wearing faded blue jeans—just to underscore their poverty. The woman is carrying a baby. They oooh and ahhhh at your furniture, your paintings, the avocado-colored refrigerator. "Gosh," says the wife, "what a roomy house! Especially compared to our one-room basement flat next to the railroad. And we love that collection of 1960s *National Enquirers* in your basement! What an imaginative thing to collect! Darling, do you think we could scrape up $85,000? I know that our limit was $70,000, but what if we beg uncle to lend us some more money? What if I get a third job as a go-go dancer? Maybe we should put little Muffy here up for adoption?"

Answer: Say, "Well, I like you people a whole lot, and I'm going to give you a special break. You can keep the *National Enquirer* collection when I sell the house.

Actually, they were left here by the previous owner, and I've always wondered about him. But I really need $115,000, not a penny less. Have you thought of a condo? Much cheaper. Is your rich uncle looking for a house? This would be a steal for him."

If you really want to be charitable, give to the United Way, not just to one all-American couple. Besides, a contribution to the United Way may be tax deductible. In any case, the charming couple are probably real-estate sharks, planning to sell your house quickly for an obscene profit, if they can buy it from you cheap.

□ A man drops by (or phones) and offers you $80,000. "Here's my name and number," he says coolly, handing you a card. "Call me if you want to deal."

Two possibilities. One—He's a bargain hunter, and every once in a while he encounters a disturbed or desperate seller and buys a house cheap. Real-estate authority Tony Hoffman, author of *How to Negotiate Successfully in Real Estate*, knows someone who regularly offers to buy houses at 25 percent off the selling price. He's successful often enough to make a living just by reselling those houses for what they are really worth.

Two—The buyer is softening you up for the next buyer, a confederate, who may offer you $90,000. That may seem strangely attractive in contrast to $80,000.

Put the man, and his offer, out of your mind. Hand his card back to him.

□ The buyer has offered $90,000, then $92,000, then $93,000, then $93,500. You've gone down from $115,000 to $110,000. Now what do you do?

Answer: You're dealing with a knowledgeable negotiator, and he's winning. His price concessions have been smaller and smaller ($2,000, $1,000, $500). And while he's raised his bids by only a total of $3,500, you've come down by $5,000. Stay where you are until he raises his bid to $95,000—breaking his pattern of diminishing concessions by a leap of $2,500.

You should not have made any price concessions at all, in any event, until he was at $95,000, because your minimal acceptable price—$105,000— is halfway between $95,000 and $115,000.

Your own price concessions while negotiating should follow that buyer's pattern, such as going from $115,000 to $113,000 (a $2,000 drop), to $112,000 ($1,000), to $111,500 ($500). Progressively smaller price concessions lower the other negotiator's expectations.

□ The buyer says, "My final offer is $102,000. Take it or leave it."

Answer: "My final offer" and "Take it or leave it" are known as killers. They are powerful and dangerous.

Ignore them and continue bargaining. You might talk about giving the buyer the lawn mower free of charge, or paying for a termite inspection (which, in your area, might actually be your obligation). Bear in mind that $102,000 is not far from your bottom figure, $105,000. So keep plugging.

□ The buyer says, "Be reasonable. I've come up from $90,000 to $96,000. You've come down from $115,000 to $110,000. I've raised the ante $6,000 and you've lowered it by only $5,000. Let's split the difference. The middle price between $110,000 and $96,000 is $103,000. How about it?"

Answer: "Be reasonable" and "Let's split the difference" are also killers. Your response to the first should be, "I've thought about it very carefully, and I'm absolutely certain that I *am* being reasonable." Your response to the second: "I can't afford to split the difference." (Pleading poverty is always a wise tactic.)

In this case, while the buyer has raised his bids by $6,000 and you've dropped by only $5,000, he started out low—at $90,000. But a $103,000 bid is in the ballpark. Consider matching his concessions above $95,000 ($8,000) by dropping to $107,000.

□ "All cash—$100,000," says the buyer. "You choose the moving date. How about it? I'll sign a binder right now. Do you have a pen?"

Answer: While the offer is below your minimum, it's unusually appealing. "Cash up front" is one of the most beautiful phrases in the English language. At least be encouraging. You might lower your price a bit, or make some other sort of concession. For example, you might offer to pay the remainder of the house insurance for the rest of the year—if it's late in the year. You won't have to wait to receive a refund, which usually isn't much anyway because of service charges.

□ "I'm deciding between your house and two others. I'll be forced to eliminate yours unless you bring the price down to $100,000."

Answer: Clever buyers always remind you of the competition—castles supposedly on sale for a song. Remind this buyer that he has competition, too—buyers with bulging moneybags.

You might say, "Well, I hope you won't eliminate my house from consideration. But I'm probably making a mistake by offering it to you for less than $115,000, which is what brokers told me they could sell it for." Then remind the buyer that others will be looking at your house; you have more advertisements scheduled to run; you're holding another open house.

Once, while buying a house, I offered $70,000; the seller wanted $80,000. "You're pretty far apart," the broker said to me sadly. "What shall we do?" In front of the seller, I said, perfectly honestly, "Let's see that house on Howe Avenue again—the one selling for $68,000."

The seller got a little nervous, and sold. me the house for $71,000.

Don't get nervous, especially if your house has not been on the market long. Be prepared to test whether a buyer is bluffing.

□ Says the buyer, "I figure your house is worth $105,000. Subtracting half a broker's fee, at 7 percent, would bring it to $101,325. I'll give you $102,000."

Answer: Who is he to decide the value of your house? Your response might be, "Brokers tell me the house is worth $115,000. Subtracting half a broker's fee—and the broker I have in mind would charge only 6 percent— would bring it down to $111,550. But that wouldn't pay me for the advertisements I've bought, and the time I've spent answering the phone and showing people around the house. I've *earned* the broker's fee. But I'm willing to be reasonable. I'll sell for $110,000 if the other terms are good."

□ "My wife hates Colonials—all those stairs!" says the buyer. "And she wants walk-in closets, an in-ground swimming pool, a great big entrance foyer, a kitchen with two ovens and a microwave, and Tibetan rugs. Personally, I love your house and everything about it. The parquet floors, the fireplace, the suede wallpaper, even those avocado-colored appliances in the kitchen. Maybe I could bring her around if she felt the price was right . . . $90,000, maybe."

Answer: Clever. He's the good guy, she's the bad guy,

and the two of you should work together to win her over. But two can play at this game.

You might reply, "My spouse is unhappy about selling for less than $115,000, and I'm not sure he would accept even $112,000. Anyway, bring your wife around and I'll tell her about the great shopping areas, the social life, how good stair climbing is for aerobic conditioning, and how low heating and cooling costs are in a Colonial. And if her heart is set on a microwave oven, I'll buy her one as a housewarming gift. Believe me, she'll be easier to persuade than my husband. Last night, he was thinking of raising the price to $120,000!"

□ The couple ask you about the schools, the shopping, the electrical capacity of the house, whether the fireplace equipment stays. Then one of them says, "Would you come down a bit on the price?"

Answer: There's a strong tug on your fishing line. Say, "I'll come down for reasonable terms—if you have financing, a good credit record, a good move-in date. What can you afford? Maybe we can work something out." You've already given a price—$115,000. Wait until they name a price before making any concessions.

□ The couple look over the house thoroughly, ask lots of questions, then come back a second time. "Would you accept $105,000?"

Answer: Be encouraging. If your house has just been put on the market, you should probably haggle a bit. But be careful not to lose them. Don't be greedy. You might say, "That's a little low, but maybe we can work something out. You know, I'm thnking of throwing the appliances into the deal. How about if I brought the price down a bit—to maybe $112,000?"

132

□ The couple examine the house thoroughly, ask a lot of questions, and offer $114,000.

Answer: "Would you put that in writing? It's pretty close to my selling price, and I'll seriously consider it."

□ Says the buyer, "I'll give you $75,000—if you'll sign a note to take back some paper—and I'll throw in my recreational vehicle worth $25,000, plus a vacation lot in Utah worth $5,000, and a 1976 Capri Classic worth $6,000. That amounts to $111,000. How about it? I need your answer right now. I'm dickering with some people up the block—they're test driving the recreational vehicle now, which is why you can't see it. Will you accept my check for $50 as a binder?"

Answer: Show him the door. Any complicated deal should scare you off. Keep things simple.

□ Says the buyer, "What's your rock-bottom price? We can save a lot of time if you tell me. We may be able to knock out a deal in the next ten minutes."

Answer: Don't tell him. If you say $105,000, you've made a $10,000 concession—and the bargaining may start from there. He might respond, "Well, my top offer is $95,000. Why don't we split the difference and settle on $100,000?"

What you might reply: "Well, I'm glad you're interested. And the $115,000 is negotiable. My price will depend on the financing, the move-in date, what items I leave, and what I take with me. I'm not sure what my rock-bottom price is. What's your top price?"

□ Buyer: "A house down the block just went for $95,000—and it has five bedrooms and a swimming pool. How can you offer yours for $115,000 when it has only three bedrooms and no swimming pool?"

Answer: If you don't know anything about this alleged house with five supposed bedrooms and swimming pool that reportedly went for $95,000, just say, "Wow, what a bargain! I'm glad I called in some smart people to give me a *reliable* estimate on what my house is worth."

Ideally, though, you'll be able to respond: "The owner lost his job and was desperate." Or, "The basement is always flooding, the house needs a new roof, and the bedrooms are the size of postage stamps. Isn't it worth $20,000 more to have a house with a dry basement, a roof in good condition, and three *spacious* bedrooms? Besides, in the past fifty years there have been six murders in that house."

☐ The buyer bid $105,000, but now he phones and says, "I've been thinking about your strange wallpaper and checking my finances. I can only offer $100,000."

Answer: You're dealing with someone slippery. If you waste more time with him, he'll probably come up with other cute tricks. For example, he may finally offer $108,000, then come to the closing with a check for only $100,000—and tell you to take it or leave it. Just say, "Good luck on buying the house you can afford."

As one noted negotiator has said, "The first time someone tries to screw you, he's only practicing."

Don't give him a second chance.

THE CASE FOR BARGAINING

"Americans," the anthropologist E. T. Hall once observed, "tend to look down upon people who haggle."

Another anthropologist, Joy Brown, author of *The Used Car Game*, claims that—in the public's mind—bargaining is "the process carried on between an unsavory, robe-wrapped charlatan and an unsuspecting American tourist complete with camera and flowered sport shirt."

Yet haggling—or, if you prefer, "bargaining" or "negotiating"—is all but essential when you buy or sell a house in most parts of the country.

It's all but essential not just because it's traditional, but because it's wise.

When a product or service is expensive—say, $115,000—sellers are usually willing to drop their prices a bit. And when a product or service is desirable, buyers are usually willing to raise their offers a bit.

Take a house with a selling price of $115,000. A buyer wants to pay $110,000. The difference is $5,000—a good piece of change.

Yet, from another point of view, the difference is not that much; $115,000 is only 4.5 percent more than $110,000. It's comparable to the difference between $1 and $1.05. A seller and a buyer would probably not pay that much attention to a nickel's difference between them, yet naturally they're concerned about $5,000. But it would be foolish for them to believe that the spread is so enormous that they cannot compromise. The bargaining process, in fact, facilitates many exchanges between buyers and sellers who might otherwise have passed by like ships in the night.

Now, for every house, there's probably a Perfect Buyer. Your house, and everything about it, enchants him and miraculously fulfills all of his needs and those of his family, from the number of bedrooms to the closeness of workplaces. If the Perfect Buyer has the wherewithal, he should pay top dollar.

Then there's the Imperfect Buyer. Your house is not absolutely wrong for him, but it's not quite right for him, either. He was hoping for an extra bedroom for an office, he is unhappy about the long commute to his place of business, or the price is simply more than he wanted to spend. So he probably won't meet your offering price. But if you were willing to bargain, and lower your price, you would begin to seize his attention.

In short, the final selling price of your house depends to a large extent on where any serious bidder stands in the continuum between the Perfect Buyer and the Imperfect Buyer.

Alas, there are more Imperfect Buyers around than Perfect Buyers because (1) few houses, apart from true mansions, enchant all buyers and (2) the more enchanting your house, the higher the price you probably put on it, and the fewer people who can afford it. This doesn't mean that Perfect Buyers aren't lurking out there in the bushes, waiting to pounce. It just means that, to get your top price, you may have to be very lucky. Chances are that you'll wind up selling your house to any one of a variety of Imperfect Buyers for less than top dollar.

Other factors besides luck determine the selling price, of course, such as whether the residential real-estate market is lively or stagnant, how readily buyers can obtain cheap mortgage money, the season of the year, and *how skilled the buyer and seller are at bargaining.*

If the very notion of bargaining over money nauseates you and you're in a hurry to move, you might set a somewhat low price tag on your house and call it "firm" in advertisements you publish. But you might be parting with easy money. The Perfect Buyer, perfectly willing to pay more than your low price, may have been eagerly waiting for just your ad to appear. And an Imperfect Buyer may never see your house because the "firm" price scares him, and he figures you won't budge at all.

So, in general, don't call a price "firm" unless you really mean it.

And be prepared to negotiate.

Price Isn't Everything

Gerald I. Nierenberg, a lawyer who wrote *The Art of Bargaining*, likes to tell audiences that he will buy anyone's watch for, oh, $1,000. Naturally, several people pass him their $19.95 Timexes.

Then Nierenberg explains the other terms of the deal, besides the price: He will pay them 1 cent toward the $1,000 price—every time they happen to run into each other in Timbuktu.

In other words, the $1,000 will be paid to them awfully slowly, and in awfully tiny installments.

Now that these naive people have learned their lesson—"Price isn't everything"—Nierenberg returns their watches.

The price you want for your house is vital, of course. Just don't overlook the other terms.

□ Does the buyer have his own money or a mortgage, or does he intend to borrow from you? Might the deal fall through if he can't get a mortgage for the amount he needs, at the miraculously low interest rate he specifies?

□ Does he want the contract to specify that if a house engineer finds any trivial defect at all he can back out? (See the discussion on contingencies in Chapter 13.)

□ Does he agree with you on what stays with the house, and what you take with you?

□ Is he willing to put down a sizable amount as a binder, or does he insist on just $100?

Certainly, above all you want your asking price. But if

137

you find a buyer who has money or a mortgage, who is willing to sign a firm contract, and who is accommodating about everything else—the move-in date, the items that stay or go—you could lower your price a little.

Price isn't everything.

Money Isn't Everything

By the same token, you might induce a buyer to raise his offer if you make concessions—even if these concessions don't lower your asking price. You could volunteer to throw in the appliances, the lawn mower, the patio furniture. You could offer to pay for something inexpensive—buy a microwave oven, have a cleaning woman make the house spotless after you move out.

Buyers always seem to imagine that something costs more than it really does, whether it's replacing a cracked windowpane or having a living room repainted. By offering to pay for such items, you may salvage a deal that might otherwise have flown out the window.

These concessions work both ways. You can withhold them if the buyer refuses to raise his offer. "Well, if you're not going to go over $105,000, I'll have to sell the appliances and the patio equipment—or take them with me."

Use Your Imagination

In 1947, Gerard B. Lambert, who had made a fortune in pharmaceuticals, put his 500-acre Virginia estate up for sale for $275,000. A wealthy coal-mine owner agreed to meet the price. At the last minute, there was a disagreement. The miner wanted to buy a Gilbert Stuart painting of George Washington that hung in the house's foyer. Lambert refused to part with it, even for $25,000.

138

The real-estate agent suggested that they toss a coin. They did. The coal-mine owner won—and the house was sold.

Don't Be Antagonistic

Don't let the bargaining process turn into something resembling a duel to the death. Chat with the buyer about other things—hobbies, families. Give buyers helpful advice, such as the names of a good carpenter and plumber. Suggest that they can save on the cost of title insurance if they use the same company you used.

Antagonism can sour a deal. Both of you may become irrationally stubborn about minor concessions; you may wind up disliking each other so much that you simply cannot do business together.

Don't Be Inflexible

If the real-estate market seems to be in the doldrums, if your phone hardly rings except for calls from hungry real-estate agents, if buyers coolly walk in and out of your house without comment, be prepared to pay attention to offers below your target selling price.

Don't Let Your Ego Get Involved

In experiments, college professors auction off dollar bills. Some people wind up bidding more than a dollar—just to win the auction.

Don't let your ego get so involved in the bargaining that you would feel humiliated if you accepted a little less than you wanted. If your rock-bottom price is $110,000 and someone refuses to budge over $108,500, don't throw him out the door. It's worth something not to spend more money on ads, more time with buyers. It's worth something to *sell* your house, and not wonder when it might sell. Think about telling the man with the $108,500 offer, "Okay, you win. It's $108,500—I really want to get out. But do *me* a favor now. Let's move up the closing and move-in dates."

Max H. Bazerman, a professor at the J. L. Kellogg Graduate School of Management, Northwestern University, describes this situation:

You bought a house a few years ago for $60,000. Now you're offering it for $105,000, but would settle for $100,000. A buyer bids $90,000. Is this a $10,000 loss (from your $100,000 rock-bottom price) or a $30,000 gain (above your $60,000 purchase price)? If you think of it as a gain, you'll be more likely to accept.

If you ever catch yourself being stubborn over a relatively small amount of money, perhaps you are looking at the transaction through the wrong end of the telescope.

Time Is of the Essence

If you are to be well paid for the time you spend selling your own house, you must not squander that time. And some clever buyers may induce you to do just that.

A buyer may inspect your house, and indicate that he will meet your $115,000 price. He talks about closing dates and move-in dates. He inquires about schools and shopping. He may inspect the house a second time, with his wife; and a third time, with his friends. Then he makes one more appointment to check over the house, just to make sure. You don't really mind because, obviously, he's about to buy.

Then, having raised your hopes and dissipated a lot

of your time, he says, "Well, I've decided to offer $100,000—that's all I can afford."

Of course you'll be annoyed. But, thinking about all the time you've wasted on him, and perhaps being a bit depressed because your hopes have been dashed, you may be tempted to give in.

Just keep in mind that he's wasted *his* time, too—unless the deal goes through. Stick to your original selling price.

And, in the future, husband your time.

Don't Get Carried Away

Good books about bargaining are readily available: *Give & Take* by Chester L. Karrass, and the already mentioned *How to Negotiate Successfully in Real Estate* by Tony Hoffman, to name just two.

But don't take everything you read as gospel. Among the advice you may encounter:

☐ Always arrive late at a negotiating session—by 5 to 7 minutes.

☐ Watch the other person's eyes. If he blinks a lot, supposedly the subject is important. (If he blinks 4-8 times a minute, it's normal—unless he's wearing contact lenses, in which case 8-12 blinks is normal. If he blinks 20-30 times a minute, the subject is *very* important.)

☐ If a person is lying, his pupils will become smaller—and you will notice if you are within 5 feet of him. (If you yourself plan to lie, do it outside, in the sunlight, so your pupils are small to begin with.)

JUST KEEP IN MIND . . .

Start with a somewhat high selling price, and come down by progressively smaller amounts. Remember that both you and the buyer can make concessions involving items other than cash. Don't let a near-deal escape, especially if you have had your house on the market for a while without any encouragement. Be wary of dealing with anyone you don't trust, or anyone who suggests anything very unusual—like trading something other than old-fashioned money for your house.

A GUIDE TO MORTGAGES AND TRUST DEEDS

12

Because you are selling your house without an agent, no doubt you are an unusually self-reliant and self-confident human being. Just don't start getting uppity. Accept the fact that complex mortgage financing is probably beyond you—just as it is beyond most agents, and even beyond many lawyers. When a smiling buyer begins talking about your "taking back some paper," or the "rich uncle program," or the "triple nickel mortgage," get help.

One charming crook hopscotches around the country looking for houses to live in—free, or almost free, of charge. He scans newspapers for houses that have been advertised for months, figuring that their owners are getting desperate. He calls the owners, inspects the house, and ostensibly falls madly in love. And he's so wealthy he will pay full price. Unfortunately, he happens to be a bit cash poor right now, what with some trouble he's been having selling an apartment complex out of state, for $7 million. Would the sellers accept a token down payment and give him a mortgage? His charm and his nerve carry the day.

When the charming crook falls behind on the mortgage payments, he stalls the sellers. Unexpected problems. Not to worry.

When the sellers finally haul him into court to foreclose, they discover that the process can take three years and cost $10,000.

This particular crook, who was last seen fleecing a physician in Florida, ran rings around the real-estate agent and the lawyer who were advising the poor doctor. He has boasted that on occasion he has managed to live in houses free of charge *for years.*

The lesson, which I shall repeat, is: Be very leery of unusual mortgage terms. Be dubious about lending any buyers any money. And remember that the most successful con people have not only your trustfulness working for them; they also tend to be among the most charming people on the entire planet.

I'll have more ugly things to say about "creative financing"—where the seller helps the buyer financially—later on. But a word of reassurance: In many states west of the Mississippi, houses are sold by means of trust deeds rather than mortgages. A trustee (often an escrow agent) holds the deed until the borrower (the trustor) fulfills the contract. If the borrower defaults, foreclosure can be quick and sure. And in such states, seller financing is not quite so perilous as is in those states where mortgages are the rule.

Let's look at some other aspects of mortgages before returning to creative financing.

SHOULD YOU LET A BUYER ASSUME YOUR MORTGAGE?

Yes—if it will help you sell your house and if you are careful. Besides, if a buyer takes over your mortgage kit and kaboodle, you won't have to face a "prepayment penalty"—a charge of a few hundred dollars the lender may hit you with for paying off your mortgage early. (Some 18 percent of conventional—that is, nongovernment—mortgages assess prepayment penalties if the mortgage is closed out before five years have elapsed.)

Smart buyers are eager to assume mortgages. They can save over a thousand dollars in normal closing costs— on title insurance, an appraisal, a survey, loan origination fees, and so forth.

Mortgage assumptions are not quite so tempting as they once were, simply because interest rates have come down. Your old mortgage probably doesn't have an exceptionally low interest rate. And even if it does, there may not be much left to pay off. Still, any mortgage you have that is assumable will make your house a shade more attractive than a similar house down the street. Mention your "assumable mortgage" on your fact sheet.

If you have a Federal Housing Administration-insured mortgage, or a Veterans Administration-guaranteed mortgage, it is automatically assumable— even if the buyer isn't a veteran.

145

Only a minority of conventional loans are assumable: perhaps 25 percent. More variable-rate mortgages are assumable than fixed-rate mortgages (the rate on variable-rate mortgages moves up and down in accordance with an economic indicator of interest rates, like 90-day Treasury bills). Most mortgages have legally enforceable "due on sale" clauses, which specify that if you sell your house you must pay off the balance of the mortgage. But check with your lawyer to see whether your own mortgage has an enforceable "due on sale" clause.

Shrewd buyers will be especially interested in assuming an adjustable-rate mortgage if it has a ceiling on rate increases—and the ceiling has been reached. At that point, the rate can only go down.

Warning: If a buyer assumes your mortgage, make sure that the lender does not hold you accountable if the buyer defaults. You want to be completely out of the picture. Your agreement with the lender must make the buyer totally responsible for the mortgage in the future. If you give the buyer a second mortgage at the same time he or she assumes your first mortgage, have the lender agree to inform you if the buyer begins falling behind on payments. At least you will have more time to consider what steps to take if the buyer begins to default.

SHOULD YOU ACCEPT AN OFFER CONTINGENT ON A GOVERNMENT-BACKED MORTGAGE?

The conventional wisdom is that nonconventional mortgages—those backed by the FHA or the VA—are bad news for sellers. Supposedly such mortgages take almost forever for approval; the VA and the FHA may require repairs that their appraisers recommend; and, worst of all, you yourself may have to pay points (loan charges) that the lending institution assesses—each point equaling 1 percent of the loan.

Actually, mortgages backed by the FHA or VA aren't so terrible. Sometimes buyers get approval fairly quickly. If you must make repairs, well, at least you won't have to worry that the buyer will haul you into court later on. As for the points, with FHA-backed mortgages, you can negotiate with the buyer, and, while you must pay the points for VA-backed mortgages, many sellers simply raise their selling prices to cover the cost.

In any case, if you sell your house to a buyer with a nonconventional mortgage, you almost always get your full asking price. You'll probably wind up making more than you would if you accepted an offer from a buyer with a conventional mortgage.

Neither the FHA nor the VA actually issues mortgages. They insure (FHA) or guarantee (VA) a percentage of a mortgage. The FHA will usually insure a mortgage up to $67,500, but will go as high as $90,000 in high-priced housing areas, like San Diego. The down payment the FHA requires is 3 percent of the first $25,000 plus 5 percent of the amount over $25,000. (The down-payment requirement may soon rise to 5 percent of the total for families with more than $40,000 in income.)

Buyers love government-backed mortgages because (1) they require small down payments, or none at all, and (2) their interest rates are almost always lower than rates on conventional mortgages.

The VA guarantees 60 percent of a mortgage, or $27,500, whichever is less (but will not guarantee even $27,500 if the mortgage exceeds $110,000). The buyer need not make any down payment. If the buyer does, though, he can obtain a mortgage as high as $135,000.

147

Before putting their houses on the market, some sellers call in a VA-approved appraiser, just to speed up a sale in case a veteran comes along.

SHOULD YOU GIVE BUYERS ADVICE ABOUT MORTGAGES?

Certainly. As a homeowner, you probably know more about the subject than the typical buyer knows simply because many have never owned homes.

To begin with, as mentioned, check what size mortgage local lenders will offer on your house, at what interest rate, and for what term. (A mortgage for 30 years is common, but a 15-year term will shrink enormously the total interest that buyers will pay. And with tax reform, the deductible interest isn't so valuable anymore.)

Tell buyers that a fixed-rate mortgage is usually better if they plan to live in your house for a long time because it will be easier on their long-range budgeting. An adjustable-rate mortgage almost always has a lower interest rate, at its inception; if the buyers plan to live in your house only a few years, then this type of mortgage may make sense.

On their own, the buyers should investigate mortgages they can obtain. They should shop various institutions (savings and loan associations, mortgage brokers, credit unions), both in and out of town. The better newspapers now list the terms of various mortgages in the areas the papers cover; independent mortgage specialists are also springing up, like HSH Associates in Riverdale, New Jersey, which publishes a newsletter comparing mortgage rates and terms in the East.

SHOULD YOU EVER HELP THE BUYER WITH THE FINANCING?

Only under exceptional circumstances: You might not sell the house readily if you don't; the buyers are unusually trustworthy; and you have the guidance of an unusually competent and knowledgeable lawyer, perhaps along with a mortgage lender.

All right, all right. A knowledgeable real-estate agent can be valuable if you're contemplating giving a buyer a mortgage. You can hire one on a consulting basis. Look for an agent listed in *Who's Who in Creative Real Estate*, obtainable for $25.00 plus $2.40 for handling from *Who's Who*, P.O. Box 23265, Ventura, CA 93002 (you'll also receive a list of agents who represent buyers, not sellers; see Chapter 16).

But be careful. Seller financing is dangerous, even if the buyers aren't crooks intent on living in your house rent-free. They might instead be the kind of crooks who buy your house, then sell it to innocents who don't know that the place is mortgaged. (They could have learned as much by checking the "recorder's office" in your area, where your mortgage would have been open for public inspection.) Or they may be the kind of crooks who manage to borrow more than the house is worth—through first, second, third, and even fourth mortgages—from you as well as mortgage lenders. And then they sneak off into the night with their profit.

Or they may not be crooked but honest, decent, upright people who just cannot continue paying your mortgage. And because they have so little invested in the house (their down payment was tiny), they simply walk away. Sure, you get your house back. But because the buyers were too poor to pay your mortgage, they may not have paid the real-estate taxes. Also, they almost certainly didn't call in plumbers, electricians, roofers, glaziers, and others to repair anything that went wrong. And they themselves may have been too busy trying to earn extra money to keep the place clean and well running. Your once-beautiful house is probably a shambles now. The damage that careless tenants can do to a house is appalling, but I shall spare you my own tale of woe.

Well, what if you give the buyers a mortgage for only $5,000? They certainly won't walk away from that. On the other hand, they may be shrewd enough to know that if you sold your house in Minnesota and moved to Hawaii, you may not be enthusiastic about the prospect of returning to sue for $5,000 when a foreclosure may cost $10,000. In fact, the buyers may religiously repay you $45,000 of a $50,000 mortgage they owe you—then stop right there.

No wonder Garth Marston, author of the book *Creative Real Estate Financing*, warns: "Seller financing is generally not a good idea. Most of us have neither the time nor the skill to manage such an investment successfully, nor the wherewithal to back us up if something goes wrong."

Fortunately, seller financing isn't as common now as it was in 1982, when mortgage money was scarce and 25 percent of all home sales required owner financing. Today, mortgage money is readily available; only 8 percent of sellers give a first mortgage, only 5 percent a second mortgage—and many of *them* may be selling mansions, which typically entail seller financing.

If you ever decide to give a first or second mortgage (that is, "take back some paper"):

◻ Ask for a 20 percent down payment. When the

150

Federal National Mortgage Association (Fannie Mae), which buys mortgages, studied 5,000 cases of foreclosure, it found that loans with down payments of 10 percent to 19 percent were three times riskier than loans with down payments of 20 percent or more; loans with down payments of less than 10 percent were five times riskier.

☐ Try to work with a lender who can obtain mortgage insurance for you—even if yours is a second mortgage. The lending institution will run a credit check on the buyer, then have you and the buyer fill out standard mortgage forms. After you lend the buyer the money, the professional lender will service the loan (collect the monthly payments and perhaps put aside money for taxes), and obtain insurance for you in case the buyer defaults, covering up to $107,000 (the highest mortgage that Fannie Mae will purchase). The insurance also covers the cost of a foreclosure. A professional lender may charge loan-origination fees along with .5 percent or .75 percent of the total mortgage.

☐ Try to limit the term of the mortgage (especially a second mortgage) to only three to five years. That way, you will get your money sooner, and, if you want to sell the mortgage, it will be worth more. (Usually you can sell a mortgage only at a hefty discount, such as 20 percent.) But be warned that in certain states, like Massachusetts, if a mortgage has a "balloon" (the entire amount comes due after a few years, even though the payments were based on a longer period), the seller must offer the buyer a new mortgage.

☐ Try to live in a state in which trust deeds, not mortgages, are traditional. Or try to have your lawyer work out a "contract of sale," in which the title doesn't change hands until a full down payment has.

Once upon a time, there was a special benefit to seller financing: You didn't have to report all your capital gains in just one year. Instead, because you were in effect arranging an "installment sale," you could spread the taxes on your capital gains over a few years. But the Tax Reform Act of 1986 has severely curtailed the tax benefits of installment sales.

WHAT ELSE SHOULD I, AS A SELLER, KNOW ABOUT MORTGAGES?

Some terms you should be familiar with:

Wraparound. The buyer obtains a secondary mortgage from you, but you continue paying your first mortgage. This may be advantageous if your own mortgage has a low interest rate, but if the lender finds out, and there's a "due-on-sale" clause in your mortgage, the arrangement may be quashed.

Bridge Loan. A short-term loan (12 to 18 months) that enables you to put a down payment on another house before you have sold your own. Not many lenders offer such loans, and the fees vary tremendously, so shop around.

Blend Loan. You have an old, low-interest mortgage; your lender, to get it off the books, agrees to give your buyer a mortgage that blends current interest rates with the rate on your old mortgage.

Okay, it's test time.

A buyer offers you $100,000 for your house; the buyer already has approval on a mortgage, and will make a 20 percent down payment.

Another buyer offers you $120,000 for your house—if

you will accept a mere $5,000 down payment, and give the buyer a $115,000 mortgage.

Which is preferable?

Answer: It's not as simple as you may think. If you have to sell that $115,000 mortgage, you may receive 80 percent of the amount—$92,000. That, plus $5,000, is $97,000 . . .

SIGNING ON THE DOTTED LINE

CONTINGENCIES CAN KILL

13

If a buyer is willing to purchase your house but insists on writing into the contract certain peculiar-sounding conditions, phone your lawyer. You may be dealing with a sharpie.

If a buyer makes his purchase contingent on vague or unenforceable conditions, he has, in effect, wangled an option on your house. Your house isn't sold; it cannot be sold to anyone else. It's a halfway house.

The buyer may have one or two goals in mind. Perhaps he just wants more time to ruminate. This is unfair because, meanwhile, your house is off the market.

Or perhaps the buyer is hoping that you will stop showing your house, put a deposit on another house, start packing everything into boxes, make arrangements with a moving company, and confidently await the day of the closing. Then, while the buyer stalls, you will become anxious and worried. Finally, when the buyer says he can afford to pay $15,000 less than the agreed-upon price, out of desperation you may capitulate.

I myself have used conditional clauses to extricate myself from possible purchases.

Once, on a purchase contract (binder), I wrote, "Subject to a satisfactory report from a housing engineer." The engineer came, saw, and said the basement leaked. The sellers, alarmed, offered to buy me the best sump pump on the market. I told them that I simply refused to own a home with a leaky basement. And a house with a wet basement, I went on, was not what I had in mind by the word "satisfactory."

Actually, I had decided that the house was charming but too small—and the leaky basement simply confirmed my resolve not to buy.

But don't become neurotic about contingency clauses.

Some conditions are acceptable, like "Subject to review by my lawyer." If you don't let the buyers show the contract to their lawyer and the matter winds up in court, you have hurt your case.

Some conditions can be dealt with. Let's say that the buyers want to buy your home, conditional upon their selling their own home. You can add your own condition: You will continue showing the house, and, if you find a second buyer, they will have 48 hours to remove their contingency clause. Or, more leniently, if they do not sell their home within 60 days, you can start showing your home again.

And some conditions can kill—buyers. In West Virginia, a couple agreed to purchase a house for $77,000, "subject to the approval of financing." They visited a bank, which appraised the property at $68,000 and offered to lend the buyers 80 percent of $68,000. The buyers apparently were miffed at buying the house for $9,000 more than its appraisal, so they informed the sellers that the deal was off.

The sellers sued, and won. They had finally sold the house to another buyer for $63,000, but the first buyers had to pay them the difference between the price they had offered and the final sales price—$14,000.

An appeals court upheld the verdict: "Although the phrase 'subject to the approval of financing' is far from specific, it is not so indefinite or devoid of meaning as to void the contract . . . . The buyer must make reasonable, good faith efforts to obtain financing."

The best way to deal with contingency clauses is to run them past your lawyer. But, in general, make sure that all contingencies have time limits; that they are realistic; that they spell out what will happen if the condition is *not* met.

What if the buyers want the sale conditional upon their obtaining a mortgage at an interest rate 2 points below the going rate? Refuse. They can seek a mortgage at the prevailing rates, for the usual length of time (25 years), for the usual amount of money (80 percent of the appraised value of the house). And give them only 2 or 3 weeks to nail down the financing.

What about "Subject to a satisfactory report from a housing inspector"? Fine, if there's a time limit (say, 2 weeks) and if you spell out in the contract how any defects will be remedied. (Either you will have all defects repaired, or you and the buyer will share the cost.

SELL YOUR OWN HOME

Or you will get an estimate of the cost of repairs, and lower the selling price by that amount.)

What if the buyer wants to move in before the closing? Check with your lawyer, but, by and large, refuse. It's rarely a good idea to let someone into your house before the title has changed hands. Evicting someone can be murder. Besides, the buyer, once inside your house, will gradually notice all sorts of flaws and imperfections— and may try to back out..

What if the buyers want a guarantee that everything in the house is in working order? Sure, you can guarantee this up to the day the title changes hands. After that, if the furnace blows up or the refrigerator dies a noisy death, they are on their own. Otherwise, you may be responsible for repairing any damage they do accidentally. (Like the buyers who had forgotten that the fireplace was only for decoration, and upon moving in lit a fire.)

BINDERS AND CONTRACTS

In some parts of the country, a "binder" (also called a "purchase offer," "tentative contract," or "memorandum of sale") is all that a buyer and seller sign. There is no carefully worded, detailed contract later on. In other parts of the country, binders are so informal that they are in effect "earnest money" receipts (earnest money being sort of a "good faith" deposit, but not an actual deposit): If either buyer or seller wants out, the deal is quashed and usually the money returned.

Depending on where you live, the handling and amount of the earnest money will vary. Sometimes the earnest money is a mere $100; sometimes it's $1,000 or more. It is usually turned over to the seller's lawyer, who keeps it in escrow. Later, the buyer must come up with a hefty deposit—usually 10 percent of the purchase price—and at the closing fork over the remainder. In some areas, if the buyer backs out for good reason (she loses a job), it's traditional for the earnest money to be returned. In other areas, the seller keeps the money.

In short, local customs govern. If you don't know how matters are handled in your area, ask your lawyer or banker or accountant—or neighbors.

A CRASH COURSE IN REAL-ESTATE LAW

Everything regarding the sale of real estate, by and large, must be in writing. A buyer who offers to pay you $1 million for your house has no obligation to do anything of the sort unless it's in writing, and her spouse has signed, too, if they will own the house jointly.

To be valid, a binder must:

- □ list the purchase price
- □ identify the property (a street address and the approximate acreage will do)
- □ specify the method of payment (when the deposit will be made, when the balance)
- □ give the names of the buyer's and seller's lawyers
- □ indicate the place and time of the closing, and the date of possession

A binder may indicate which fixtures remain with the house, such as sinks, the furnace, and the trees outside. The seller should list whatever he wants to remove— say, drapes, rugs, fireplace equipment. If an item is not mentioned and it's not clearly a fixture or a furnishing, it goes with the seller.

Typically a closing is held 30 to 60 days after the

binder is signed. If there is to be an elaborate contract, it can be signed in advance of the closing. The date of possession is usually scheduled a day or two after the closing. These dates can be moved up or down—unless a "time is of the essence" clause is inserted, stressing the importance of the specific dates.

The binder ("Offer to Purchase") shown on pages 162–163 is typical of what you can pick up in any large stationery store. It's more detailed than some, less detailed than others. Have such binders in your house, along with carbon paper, so you and the buyer can have your own copies.

The seller fills out the back, the buyer the front. Cross out anything that does not apply (such as references to a broker's commission). You and the buyers should sign your names and the date next to any such changes. The L.S. at the end means legal signature.

The blank space after the first paragraph ("Property") is for you and the buyer to list other household items that stay and those that go. The space after "Balance" is for conditions, such as "the buyer will obtain a mortgage loan for $80,000, at prevailing interest rates, with a life of 25 years or more, with monthly debt service."

The remainder of the binder is pretty easy to understand. After all, it's typically filled in by real-estate agents, not lawyers.

Your own lawyer may prefer that you use a binder agreement that she will draw up especially for you.

29 REASONS YOUR HOUSE MAY NOT BE SOLD

Just because you have a binder, earnest money, and a firm date for the closing, don't rejoice and relax. Keep showing your house, explaining the situation to visitors. Sales sometimes fall through, and for unpredictable reasons.

Here are some cases cited by Irving Price, a well-known writer and broker in upstate New York, in his book *How to Get Top Dollar for Your Home**:

1. The buyer accepted the seller's invitation to swim in his electrically heated pool, and was almost electrocuted.
2. Before the closing, the buyer's wife noticed a large black snake crawl out from beneath the home.
3. A fast-food restaurant started going up across the street.
4. The seller's dog took a big chunk out of the buyer's leg.
5. Real-estate taxes turned out to be $1,800, not $800.
6. The buyer, a CIA agent, learned that the rural phone company could not provide him with a private line.
7. The seller, before the closing, removed three antique lighting fixtures and replaced them with flashlights.
8. One evening, standing in front of the home her son and his wife were buying, the mother was mugged.
9. Prior to the closing, the seller took the outdoor toolshed away.
10. The charming home next door turned out to be a rehabilitation center for paroled rapists.
11. The buyer was kidnapped and held for ransom.
12. The buyer's down-payment check bounced.
13. Part of the seller's garage, it turned out, was on his neighbor's property.

SELL YOUR OWN HOME

B 122—Purchase offer, standard form: plain English: 9-81.

JULIUS BLUMBERG, INC.,
PUBLISHER, NYC 10013

This is a legally binding document. Consult your lawyer if you do not understand any part of it.

OFFER TO PURCHASE

TO THE OWNER OR PERSON WHO HAS THE RIGHT TO SELL THE PROPERTY DESCRIBED BELOW:

Property

I (We) agree to purchase the following property situated in the _____ of _____
County of _____, State of _____ known as _____
being a _____

(for a more detailed description of the property reference is hereby made to the deed thereof) together with all lighting, heating and plumbing fixtures, window shades, screen and storm doors and windows, if any, water heater, water meter and all fixtures and fittings belonging to or used in the operation of the property and owned by you.

Price AT THE PRICE OF _____ $ _____
Dollars, payable as follows:
Deposit $ _____ cash deposited with _____ to be held until this offer is accepted, at which time it shall become part of the purchase price, or returned if not accepted.
Balance $ _____ cash on or before _____ on passing of deed.

Searches, Taxes, Easements, Restrictions, Zoning, etc. You are to deliver to me or my attorney, at least five (5) days before closing, a forty year abstract of title and ten year search or tax receipts showing the property free and clear of all liens and encumbrances, except as herein set forth, and except building and use restrictions, pole and wire easements of record, and subject to zoning ordinance and to any taxes for local improvements not now completed.

Closing Transfer is to be completed at the office of _____
Deed on or before _____ or as soon thereafter as the abstracts can be brought to date. At that time you are to convey to me by _____ deed, good title to the property free of all liens and encumbrances, except as above set forth, subject to rights of tenants, if any.
Adjustments Interest, insurance premiums, rents, and taxes shall be pro-rated and adjusted as of _____, 19___

City, State and County Taxes shall be adjusted and apportioned on a calendar year beginning Jan. 1, and ending Dec. 31. School Taxes outside the city shall be adjusted and apportioned for the fiscal year beginning July 1st and ending the following June 30th, and Village Taxes shall be adjusted and apportioned for the fiscal year beginning June 1st and ending the last day of May following or as otherwise provided by law.

Possession Possession of premises shall be delivered on or before _____ 19___ on passing of deed

Mortgage Expenses Upon any purchase money mortgage given, I (We) agree to pay the usual mortgage tax and recording fee and Revenue stamps on bond where required.
Assignment This offer may be assigned to an individual or corporation for the purpose of holding title thereto. However, I (We) shall remain responsible for the faithful performance of the contract.
Risk of Loss The risk of loss or damage to the property by fire or other causes until the delivery of the deed is assumed by you.
Broker I (We) represent that _____ is the broker in this transaction and that no other real estate broker or agent has helped to bring about this sale.
Persons Bound This offer, when accepted shall be a binding contract. It shall bind the parties hereto and their respective executors, administrators, distributees, successors and assigns.

Dated _____, 19___ (Signed) _____ (L. S.)

Witness _____ (Signed) _____ (L. S.)

Forms may be purchased from Julius Blumberg, Inc., NYC 10013, or any of its dealers. Reproduction prohibited.

162

ACCEPTANCE

The undersigned hereby accepts this offer, agrees to sell on the terms and conditions set forth, and agrees to pay

_____the authorized agent,_____commission.

The deposit made or as much as covers the commission may be applied to payment of the commission.

Dated_____, 19____

(Signed)_____(L. S.)

Witness_____   (Signed)_____(L. S.)

Salesmen are not permitted to change the regular rates of commission.

PURCHASE OFFER

PROPERTY

Seller

Phone

Attorney

Phone

TO

Purchaser

Phone

Attorney

Phone

Dated_____, 19___

To be closed_____, 19___

163

14. The seller had said that a railroad track behind the house had been abandoned. He was wrong.
15. The seller was found to be mentally incompetent.
16. The small pond in the yard turned out to be an overflowing septic tank.
17. The seller, who had agreed to have the house painted, had it painted pink.
18. The groom's mother said that if the groom went ahead with the marriage she would have it annulled.
19. A tornado blew the house onto the adjoining property.
20. A delivery man accidentally dumped fuel oil down the water well.
21. The buyer never showed up on the day of the closing.
22. The buyer had a heart attack; the seller had a stroke.
23. The buyer had planned to read palms in the front parlor of her new home; the board of adjustment said no.
24. The buyer filed for bankruptcy.
25. The house burned to the ground.
26. The buyer's wife discovered that she was pregnant—and wanted a larger house.
27. The buyer and his wife separated, and he disappeared.
28. The seller finally learned that he, and not the buyer, had to pay off the rest of his old mortgage.
29. The seller finally learned that he, and not the buyer, had to pay the real-estate broker's commission.

CLOSING COMMENTS

The "title closing" or "settlement" is the formal affair in which the ownership of property changes hands. Closings tend to be stuffy and boring; those that aren't tend to be nightmares.

Custom dictates who attends a closing. Besides buyer and seller, there are usually lawyers, perhaps an escrow agent or a representative of a title insurance company, and (let's hope not) a real-estate agent. A closing may be held in the office of one of the lawyers, a lender, or an escrow agent. Typically it takes an hour or two.

14

PREVENTING PROBLEMS

Embed this phrase into your brain: *buyer's remorse*. It's how many buyers feel after agreeing to purchase a house: disillusioned and disgruntled. The honeymoon is over; the bloom is off the rose; Cinderella's horses have turned into mice. Buyers may suddenly suspect that they paid a king's ransom for your peasant's hovel. Or, to their unspeakable horror, they have noticed a hairline crack in the ceiling plaster.

What provokes buyer's remorse?

☐ The buyer is no longer comparing your magnificent mansion with the shanties she has been prowling through for months. Instead, the buyer now compares your house with the glowing memory of seeing it for the first time.

☐ The buyer has become all too familiar with the sterling virtues of your house—its spacious rooms, the marble fireplace, the black walnut kitchen cabinets, the bathtub big enough for two, the exquisite decorating, the English garden. He bypasses all of this, and concentrates on the trivial—the cracks in the plaster, a stuck window, a water stain on paneling.

To comfort remorseful buyers, reaffirm that theirs was a wise decision. "You've made a shrewd deal," you might say. "I'll miss the place—especially the bathtub built for two." Tell them that you're cursing yourself for not having held out for a higher price (you probably are). Tell them that you yourself are wondering whether you're moving into a lemon—or whether you're simply suffering from buyer's remorse (you probably are).

And remind the buyers what a decent, pious person you are. Hand over all the guarantees and warranties on the appliances. Take them on a house tour, showing them how to replace the filter in the furnace, how to recharge the water softener, how to open that stuck window. Send them a housewarming gift on the day of the closing.

Buyer's remorse kills many a closing. It lands some sellers in court.

Once, after presiding over a closing, my lawyer flippantly said to the happy couple who had just bought my house, "I never thought he'd get it off his hands. Ha ha!" The couple turned white. (I should have said, "Their choice in houses is much better than my choice in lawyers.")

DEALING WITH PROBLEMS

Yes, voices and fists have been raised at closings. The typical cause is a dispute over what belongs to the buyer, what belongs to the seller.

Before departing, sellers have removed bushes, chandeliers, built-in bookcases, and other amenities that buyers adored. Such conduct is a no-no, unless the sellers make adequate substitutions.

True, the line between fixtures and furnishings can be fuzzy. But, generally, a fixture is not only attached to a house but adapted for it—like wall-to-wall carpeting, drapes fitted for windows, a bookcase that occupies a stray corner. In New York State, the law is that a fixture is *screwed* in place, a furnishing *nailed*.

If there's an argument over who owns what, or who repairs what, usually might makes right. Should the sellers be confident that they can corral other buyers, or if the buyer's moving truck is smack outside the seller's house, the seller will probably emerge victorious. If the sellers have finally landed a catch after many months of fishing and if they have already moved into a new house, the buyer usually wins.

A better solution is for the lawyers to negotiate. The sellers should be prevailed upon to provide decent substitutes for items they spirited away. Also, if there has been extensive damage (from, say, a small fire), the sellers should pay for repairs. (You don't want the new buyers bad-mouthing you to all your old neighbors. It has happened.)

If the buyers seem inordinately truculent over tiny things like a missing garden plant, tell yourself: "buyer's remorse."

Another frequent problem at closings is the move-in date. The new house you are having built may not be completed; the family you bought from may not have left.

Your buyers may be magnanimous if it's a matter of a few extra days. But if the delay is a week or more, you will probably be required to pay rent, equal to a proportionate share of the mortgage and taxes as well as 10 percent on top of that. You might even have to put a few thousand into an escrow account until you finally leave.

WHO PAYS WHAT

Buyers bear the burden of closing costs—typically 6 percent of the house's selling price. (One legendary buyer, after being handed bill after bill, excused himself from a closing and was never seen again.) But sellers don't emerge scot-free.

Insist that your lawyer inform you beforehand what you must pay for. Usually the charges include recording and transfer fees, which are no big deal ($100 or so). But in your particular area you may have to pay for title insurance and escrow costs. And if the buyer has a VA or FHA mortgage (see Chapter 12), you may be required to pay points (a processing cost—each point is 1 percent of the total loan).

Happily, you should also have some money coming to you: taxes and insurance you have paid beyond the date of the closing. The buyer will also recompense you for oil you have in your tank. Prorations (yes, there is such a word) usually are made on the basis of a 360-day year with twelve 30-day months. Sellers usually pay for the closing day.

Do the buyers a favor and present them with your property survey, should you still have it. If it's less than 10 years old, they may not need to obtain a new one. Suggest that they use your old title insurance company, too; they may be entitled to a discount. (Don't pressure them, though; it's against the law, and you may be liable for three times the cost of the title policy.)

THE CONTRACT

Ideally, you and the buyer will have signed a formal contract before the closing. If disagreements are ironed out beforehand, the closing itself can be a breeze. Still, sometimes the signing of a formal contract is the center-piece of the closing.

The contract shown on pages 170–174 is for New Jersey; while it's a good model, the contracts used in your area may be markedly different.

On the first page, for example, the contract suggests that fireplace equipment, smoke and burglar alarms, and a gas barbecue grill stay with the buyer; the refrigerator, freezer, clothes washer and dryer, and window air conditioners depart with the seller. In your

M916   Contract for sale of real estate, standard form, plain language, 4-84
See form 922 for termite and building inspection clauses.

© 1984 Arthur S. Horn, a New Jersey Attorney,
Julius Blumberg, Inc., Publisher, NYC 10013

Consult your Lawyer before signing this contract — it has important legal consequences.

CONTRACT FOR SALE OF REAL ESTATE

Seller

This Contract is made and dated   19
Between:

*Address:
include
no., street,
municipality,
county,
state
and zip*

Buyer   **And**   (from now on called "the Seller")

*Address
include
no., street,
municipality,
county,
state
and zip*

                                                          · (from now on called "the Buyer")

The words "Seller" and "Buyer" include all sellers and all buyers under this Contract.

The Seller and the Buyer agree as follows:

Sale and Purchase   1. The Seller shall sell and the Buyer shall buy the Property under the terms of this Contract.

Property   2. The word "Property" in this Contract includes (a) through (d) below:

Land   (a) All of the land located in the   of
County of   and State of New Jersey, specifically described as
follows:

Street address

**Building and
Other Improvements**

All Other Rights

**Fixtures and
Personal Property**

*delete
items
not
included*

Municipal tax map designation: Lot No.   **Block No.**
(b) All buildings, driveways and other improvements on the land.
(c) All other rights of the Seller with regard to the land.
(d) All fixtures, equipment and personal property attached to or otherwise used with the land, buildings and improvements, when present at the time of the signing of this Contract, unless specifically excluded below. These are fully paid for and owned by the Seller. They include the following: plumbing, heating, electric, and cooking fixtures, electric dishwasher, hot water heater, water conditioner, lighting fixtures, TV antenna, wall to wall carpeting, fireplace equipment, smoke and burglar alarms, wall shelves, bookshelves, attached mirrors, window shades and blinds, rods and valances, storm windows and doors, window and door screens, awnings, pool equipment, garage door openers, and gas barbecue grill.

The following are excluded from this sale: furniture, household furnishings, refrigerator, freezer, clothes washer, clothes dryer, window air-conditioners, snow blower, lawn mower, and tools.

These tenancies are not in violation of any laws, rules, or ordinances. No tenant has any rights in the Property by way of option to buy, right of first refusal, pre-paid rental, or otherwise. At the closing the Seller shall give the Buyer any security deposits and interest earned as required by law.

Purchase Price and Payment *Check the paragraphs which apply and complete the blanks*

3. The purchase price is

Dollars ($

and is payable by the Buyer to the Seller as follows:

Preliminary Deposit
☐ (a) Deposit previously paid _____ $

Deposit
☐ (b) Deposit paid on the signing of this Contract, by check subject to collection _____ $

Escrow is the delivery of the deposit to a third party to be held in trust until certain conditions are met. The deposit will be held in escrow by the Seller's attorney until (1) the closing of title, at which time the deposit shall be paid to the Seller or (2) the exercise of a permitted right of cancellation under this Contract in which event the deposit shall be returned to the Buyer.

Mortgage Money
☐ (c) Money borrowed from an established lender as a first mortgage loan on the Property in the principal amount of _____ $

The Buyer shall promptly apply for this loan and use the Buyer's best efforts to obtain it. The Buyer shall supply all necessary information and fees asked for by the lender. The commitment of the lender must be received by the Buyer by   19   . The Buyer shall notify the Seller whether the commitment has been received by that date. The terms of the commitment must be at least as favorable to the Buyer as the following:
• Type of mortgage (conventional, FHA, VA, other) ___
• Annual interest rate _____   %
• Length of mortgage: years with monthly payments based on   year payment schedule.
• "Points" if any to be paid: by Buyer   by Seller
The Seller and the Buyer may later agree to extend the date for obtaining the commitment. The Buyer may accept a commitment on less favorable terms or agree to buy the Property without this mortgage requirement. If none of these events happens and the Buyer does not receive the commitment within this time period, either party may cancel this Contract.

Assumption of Mortgage
☐ (d) By the Buyer assuming the payment of the mortgage now on the Property which is held by
and has an approximate unpaid balance of _____ $
This mortgage shall be in good standing at the closing. It is payable with interest at the yearly rate of   % in monthly installments of $ The entire unpaid amount of the principal is payable on   19   Either party may cancel this Contract if the holder of the mortgage does not permit the Buyer to assume the mortgage.

Note and Mortgage to Seller
☐ (e) By a purchase money Note and First Mortgage from the Buyer to the Seller in the principal amount of _____ $
This amount shall be payable with interest at the yearly rate of   % by monthly installments of $
It shall be due in full in   years with full pre-payment rights and   day default period.
The Note, Mortgage, and Mortgagor's Affidavit of Title to be signed by the Buyer shall be prepared on standard law forms generally available in New Jersey. They shall be prepared by the Seller's attorney at the cost to the Buyer of   plus recording costs, cost of credit report on Buyer, and cost of a mortgagee policy of title insurance.

Remainder of Purchase Price
☐ (f) Remainder at closing by (i) cash (but not over 2% of the purchase price), (ii) certified check, or (iii) cashier's or other official check of a bank or savings and loan association drawn on itself. All checks must be payable to (i) the order of the Seller or (ii) the order of the Buyer and endorsed by the Buyer to the order of the Seller in the presence of the Seller. If the Buyer is a Corporation, its checks must be payable directly to the Seller _____ $ _____

Total Purchase Price _____ $

Closing of Title
4. The closing of title is the meeting at which the Seller transfers ownership of the Property by deed to the Buyer and the Buyer pays the remainder of the purchase price to the Seller. The closing of title shall take place at the office of

at _____ .M. on _____ 19____ . This is the estimated date. Either party may set a definite date by giving 10 days prior notice to the other party stating that time is of the essence. The notice cannot be served before the estimated date.

Payment of Liens

5. A lien is the claim of another against real estate for (a) the payment of money owed or (b) the performance of an obligation. Examples of liens are real estate taxes, court judgments, and mortgages. The Seller shall pay all liens against the Property in full before or at the closing. Provided that the sales price exceeds the liens, the Seller shall have the right to pay any liens on the Property at the closing from the remainder of the purchase price and if necessary from the deposit paid by the Buyer.

Condition of Property at Time of Contract

6. The Buyer has inspected the Property or has had the Property inspected by others. Except for any rights of inspection reserved in this Contract, the Buyer accepts the Property "as is." The Seller makes no statement or promise about the condition or value of the Property.

Condition of Property at Closing

7. The Seller shall transfer the Property to the Buyer in its present condition except for normal wear caused by reasonable use between now and the closing. The grounds shall be maintained. The buildings shall be in broom-clean condition. The walks and driveway shall be free of snow and ice. The Buyer may inspect the Property within 7 days before the closing on reasonable notice to the Seller.

Casualty Damage

8. The Seller is responsible for any damage to the Property except for normal usage by the Seller until the closing. If the Property is damaged by fire, vandalism, storm, flood, or any other casualty between now and the closing, the parties shall obtain an estimate from an established contractor of their choice of the cost of restoring the Property. If the estimated cost is less than 5% of the purchase price, the Seller shall (a) restore the Property before the closing at the Seller's expense or (b) deduct the estimated cost from the purchase price. If the estimated cost is more than 5% of the purchase price, the Buyer may (a) cancel this Contract or (b) proceed with the purchase, in which case the estimated cost of restoration shall be deducted from the purchase price.

Assessments for Municipal Improvements

9. Municipalities may make local improvements such as the installation of sewer systems. The cost is charged against the real estate receiving the benefit of the improvement. This charge, known as an assessment, is in addition to real estate taxes. If a municipal improvement to the Property has been completed before the date of this Contract, the Seller shall pay the assessment at or before the closing.

If a municipal improvement to the Property has not been completed before the date of this Contract, the Buyer shall pay the assessment as it becomes due.

Statements of Seller

10. The Seller makes the following statements about the Property:

(a) The Property is legally zoned for a _____ family house.

(b) The Seller has not received notice that any building or improvement is in violation of any housing, building, safety, health, or fire ordinance or law.

(c) The Property is not in a Federal or State flood hazard area.

(d) All buildings, driveways and other improvements are inside the boundary lines of the Property. There are no improvements on adjoining lands which extend onto the Property.

(e) The Seller shall obtain at the Seller's expense before the closing any certificate of occupancy or other permit if it is required by the municipality. This includes any repairs required for the issuance of the certificate.

(f) If the Property has 3 or more units of living space, the Seller shall give to the Buyer before the closing proof of compliance with the New Jersey Hotel and Multiple Dwelling Act.

The Buyer may learn before the closing that any of the statements (a) through (d) is not true and the Buyer may decide not to accept the Property under such circumstances. In that case the Buyer's only remedy is to cancel this Contract.

The Seller may not comply with statements (e) or (f) before the closing and the Buyer may decide not to accept the Property under such circumstances. In that case the Buyer's only remedy is to cancel this Contract.

Transfer of Ownership

11. The Seller shall transfer ownership of the Property to the Buyer, free of all claims and rights of others, except the following:

Utility Company Easements

(a) The rights of telephone, electric and gas, water, and sewer utility companies to maintain poles, wires, pipes, mains and cables over and under the street next to the Property, the part of the Property next to the street, or running underground directly from the street to the house on the Property.

Restrictive Covenants

(b) Limitations on the use of the Property known as restrictive covenants, provided that they (1) are not now violated, (2) do not provide that the Property would be forfeited if they were violated, and (3) do not materially restrict the normal use and enjoyment of the Property

Other Exceptions

(c)

172

In addition, the Buyer must be able to obtain title insurance on the Property from a title insurance company authorized to do business in New Jersey, subject only to the exceptions set forth in this Section.

The Buyer shall accept the transfer of ownership of the Property as it is described in this Section. However, the Seller may not be able to transfer the ownership described in this Section because of another exception which the Buyer learns of before the closing and will not accept. In that case the Buyer's only remedy is to cancel this Contract.

Transfer of Possession

12. The Seller shall transfer possession and keys of the Property to the Buyer at the closing free of all tenancies except the following:

Tenancies

Attach copy of leases

Name of Tenant	Area Rented	Lease or Month-to-Month	Monthly Rent	Security Deposit

Deed, Affidavit of Title, Realty Transfer Fee, Corporate Resolution

13. At the closing, the Seller shall transfer ownership of the Property to the Buyer by a deed of Bargain and Sale with Covenant as to Grantor's Acts. This deed contains a covenant, defined by law, that the Seller has not encumbered the Property. The deed shall be in proper form for recording. The Seller shall also give to the Buyer a sworn statement known as an affidavit of title. This affidavit shall contain information about the Seller reasonably necessary to clarify the Seller's ownership of the Property, such as (a) the Seller's marital history, (b) rights of tenants, and (c) claims on record against persons having the same or similar name as the Seller. The Seller shall pay the Realty Transfer Fee required by law. If the Seller is a corporation, it shall deliver to the Buyer at the closing a resolution of its Board of Directors approving this sale and authorizing the signing and delivery of this Contract, deed, and other closing documents by specified officers. It shall also deliver proof of any necessary shareholder approval.

Adjustment of Property Expenses

14. The parties shall apportion the following expenses relating to the Property as of the closing date according to the period of their ownership: (a) municipal real estate taxes, (b) water and sewer charges, (c) rents as and when collected, (d) interest and tax and insurance escrow on existing mortgage if assumed by the Buyer, (e) premiums on insurance policy if assumed by the Buyer, and (f) fuel oil in the tank at the price paid by the Seller. The parties shall not apportion the homestead rebate.

Broker

15. The Seller and the Buyer recognize

as the Broker who brought about this sale. The Seller shall pay to the Broker a commission of when title closes and the Buyer pays the remainder of the purchase price to the Seller.

Buyer's Lien

16. The Buyer has a legal claim known as a lien against the Property for the deposit paid and for reasonable expenses of the title search and survey. This lien shall not continue if the Buyer breaches this Contract.

Cancellation of Contract

17. In this Contract, the parties have the right to cancel this Contract under certain circumstances. In order to cancel, a party must give written notice to the other. If this Contract is so cancelled, the deposit shall be promptly returned to the Buyer. The Seller and the Buyer shall be released from all further liability to each other. However, if this Contract is cancelled because of the failure of the Seller to transfer the ownership described in Section 11, the Seller shall in addition pay the Buyer for reasonable costs of search and survey.

Notices

18. All notices given under this Contract must be in writing. They may be given by: (a) personal delivery to the other party or to that party's attorney, or (b) certified mail, return receipt requested, addressed to the other party at the address written at the beginning of this Contract or to that party's attorney. Each party must accept and claim the notices given by the other.

Assignment

19. The Buyer may not transfer the Buyer's rights under this Contract to another without the written consent of the Seller.

Full Agreement

20. This Contract is the full agreement of the Buyer and the Seller. Neither party has made any other agreement or promise that is not included in this Contract.

Changes in Contract

21. The parties may not change this Contract unless the change is in writing and signed by both parties. The parties authorize their attorneys to agree in writing to any changes in dates and time periods provided for in this Contract.

Contract Binding on Successors

22. This Contract is binding on the Seller and the Buyer and all those who lawfully succeed to their rights or take their places.

Insert termite and building inspection clauses if desired here or on a rider

173

Signatures　The Seller and the Buyer agree to the terms of this Contract by signing below. If a party is a corporation this Contract is signed by its proper corporate officers and its seal is affixed.

Witnessed or attested by:　　　　＿＿＿＿＿＿＿＿＿＿＿
　　　　　　　　　　　　　　　　　　　　Seller
＿＿＿＿＿＿＿＿＿＿＿　　　　＿＿＿＿＿＿＿＿＿＿＿
As to Seller　　　　　　　　　　　　　Seller

　　　　　　　　　　　　　　　　　　　＿＿＿＿＿＿＿＿＿＿＿
　　　　　　　　　　　　　　　　　　　Buyer
＿＿＿＿＿＿＿＿＿＿＿　　　　＿＿＿＿＿＿＿＿＿＿＿
As to Buyer　　　　　　　　　　　　　Buyer

locale, the traditions may be very different.

Overall, this contract seems eminently fair to both buyers and sellers. It allows the buyers to withdraw if they cannot obtain a mortgage on favorable terms; on the other hand, it contains an "as is" clause, which, as we have seen, is rapidly becoming a "has been" clause.

As contracts go, this one is also fairly readable; it's written, supposedly, in "plain language," despite the reference to a "deed of Bargain and Sale with Covenant as to Grantor's Acts" (number 13—leave that to your lawyer).

Read your own contract carefully and ask your lawyer any questions you may have. You should be familiar with your rights and obligations in case something untoward happens—such as the house's burning down the day after the closing (the buyer is responsible; he should already have set up the insurance and should be recompensed). And, of course, be sure that your lawyer crosses out the entire section on brokers, in particular the line, "The seller shall pay to the broker a commission of ＿＿＿＿ when title closes . . . ."

CLOSING UP SHOP

Last-minute things to do:

☐ Notify the post office of your new address.
☐ Arrange to cancel utilities (telephone, water, gas) as

of the closing day; if oil is delivered regularly, write to the company to cancel the arrangement; cancel the delivery of newspapers.

☐ Pick up any dry cleaning or laundry.

☐ Return library books.

☐ Order stationery with your new address.

☐ Send cards with your new address to friends, relatives, magazines, book clubs, insurance companies, corporations in which you own stock or whose bonds you hold.

☐ Pick up your medical, dental, and optometric records—or have them mailed to your new health specialists.

☐ Drop me a note telling me how grateful you are that I helped you sell your house without a real-estate agent.

FIZZBOS!

This chapter is one of the most important in the book. Now that you've read what a licensed real-estate salesman has to say about selling your own home, you will hear from fifteen people who have gone or are going through the process—people who sold their houses without an agent, as well as those who tried and failed.

They will tell you how they set a price for their house; how they planned the advertising campaign; how they escorted visitors through their house; how they bargained over the price and other items; and how they handled the actual signing of the contract.   Some of these fizzbos

15

are friends, or friends of friends; most are people whose phone numbers I obtained just by sifting through For Sale by Owner ads in newspapers across the country. (Some of the interviews were conducted by Elizabeth Horton and by Bram S. Boroson.)

Their advice and their experiences, you will notice, are sometimes contradictory. That may be on account of the difference in the prices of their houses, or because of differences in local customs. These fifteen come from a wide range of states: California, Illinois, Kentucky, New Jersey, New York, Rhode Island, Texas, Utah, and Washington.

Joyce Kaye, 30, bought a house in West Babylon, New York, when she was 24. "I put $1,000 down and got an FHA mortgage, all on my own," she recalls. "I was very proud of myself, a single woman buying her own house." She sold it herself recently, because, "It really wasn't the life for me out there on Long Island. It's like the 1950s there—there are mostly families, and as a single woman I felt isolated. I've always worked in Manhattan, and I have an apartment there now."

How did you set a price?

"I got an independent consultant to appraise it, someone my bank recommended. It cost $175. Then I got three Realtors to do free appraisals. Also, the consultant had showed me three houses in the area, from the outside, so I could compare them to mine. I came up with a price in the middle—$67,000."

Why did you decide to sell your house yourself?

"I lived there alone, and I wasn't going to give the keys to a Realtor to show to people while I wasn't home. So, I figured, if I'm going to have to be home anyway, why not save the commission? Why have a third party involved?"

Did your occupation help you in any way?
"I'm a contract administrator—I handle legal documents for a leasing corporation. It must have helped to some extent; I'm not intimidated by legal matters. But I'm not normally the kind of person who gets intimidated."

Did you give yourself a certain time to sell your house?
"I was very nebulous about it—I thought I'd give it a month."

Did you have a fact sheet describing your house to give to buyers?
"Yes, I had a two-page fact sheet printed, including the estimated operating expenses for a family of four; where the schools were; and special features of the house, like the two bedrooms, the totally remodeled kitchen, the new hot-water tank, the paved driveway (this is not a very rich neighborhood), the detached oversized garage, the piped-in gas instead of electricity, the sewer hookup instead of a septic tank.

"So many people were surprised that I had a fact sheet at all. Even Realtors were surprised."

What about newspaper ads?
"The first time I placed an ad, I had an open house. It didn't work. I had only put my address in the ad, with the day and time of the open house. A lot of people

came, but because my ad was so general, it was a waste of time. I hadn't included my phone number in the ad, so people came by even if they were only the least bit interested. They couldn't ask me questions about the house over the phone.

"The second time, I put my phone number in. One guy called and asked, 'Is it a Colonial?' I said no, and he hung up. He just wasn't interested in a Cape Cod, only Colonials.

"So I was able to filter people out. And in my new ad, I stressed the remodeled kitchen, the sewer hookup, the price, and 'for principals only.' It was a brief ad—three lines.

"I ran the ads for seven days each, to get a special deal from the newspaper—$120 a week."

How did you handle appointments?

"I scheduled a few people at the same time on weekends. Some took five minutes to say no, some hung around for a half-hour. I showed it to one couple during the week, because they couldn't make it on the weekend. I told all of them, 'Please call me if you can't make it,' and they were pretty good about it.

"I had bought an answering machine to get calls while I was out. It was fantastic. I couldn't have sold my house without it."

Had you spruced up your house?

"The house needed painting on the outside, but it wasn't terrible. It was in very good condition in general. I just trimmed the hedges and mowed the lawn."

Were you bothered by brokers?

"To some extent. One agent, at my open house, came to the front door, alone, and asked if I was holding an open house. Then she went back to her car and brought a couple back to see the house and get a fact sheet. And finally told me she was an agent. I thought that was underhanded.

"Other brokers would pop by, and I'd just say that I wasn't interested. If it was on the phone, I'd just hang up. If they called my answering machine, I just wouldn't call back. Fifteen different brokers contacted me."

Were people wary of buying a house directly from the seller?
"They were *thrilled*. They all had the same attitude: We all hate real-estate brokers."

How did you show people your house?
"It's a small house, so it didn't take long. I'd show them the back, take them through the house, then go to the kitchen, all the while telling them about the features, like the lovely kitchen cabinets."

Did you do anything to ensure your safety?
"I never even thought of it. It's a nice neighborhood where I live."

What about pilfering?
"I didn't have anything of value there. I guess I took a chance. Maybe I'm kind of naive. But who would steal my cigarette lighter that's also a toy train? What can I tell you?"

Any surprises?
"It went very easily. The only surprise was, people asked me questions I couldn't answer. Like whether I had 120-220 wiring. I had to look at the electrical box.

"I do know you can get into trouble if you mislead people."

Who actually bought the house?

"It was at my second open house. As soon as the woman came in, as soon as she saw the kitchen, she said, 'It fits. We can stop looking.' I knew they were serious— they asked more questions than anyone else.

"Finally they said, 'Will you take a binder?' I said yes, and called my lawyer.

"The couple weren't married yet, and this was a starter home for them.

"I probably could have gotten a few grand more. It was a very good price. Actually, I couldn't believe I was getting that much—$67,000. I was kind of lucky. Everything worked out."

How did you qualify the buyers?

"I took a chance. It was just interaction with the people. The man was in the construction field and had a lot of overtime—they really had a lot of money. He was going to apply for a mortgage strictly on his own, and expected to swing it just on his income. The woman works as a nurse. They seemed very eager, and I didn't think they'd waste their time, or mine, if they couldn't swing it. Anyway, it was a very subjective kind of thing. That's why I took a binder of only $100."

Mr. and Mrs. Richard Stone of Barrington, Rhode Island, who are in their forties, sold their house the day after they put it on the market.

Why did you decide to sell your house yourself, Mrs. Stone?

"We were familiar with the area. We had lived in Barrington for seven years, and felt we didn't need a broker. We thought selling it ourselves was worth a try. We not only sold our house without a broker, we bought one, too—just 10 miles away.

"Brokers' fees are too high. They say their fees are negotiable, but most people don't question it. They just pay 6 percent. That's a huge commission, considering our house sold for $210,000. Over $12,000. If you have a little time to play with, you can show it yourself. It's sure worth it."

Did your occupation in any way help you sell the house?

"I don't think so. My husband's an investment manager."

How did you set the price?

"We were familiar with the area, with the houses that had sold. We didn't have an appraisal. We just thought $210,000 was a fair price.

"A discount broker did look at our house, but he wasn't accustomed to houses in this price range. So he listened to what we said about the price, and his only comment was, 'Well, I think you're probably right.'

"I have a couple of broker friends who were anxious to have the house. They had said, 'Gee, when you're ready to sell, I think your house is worth X.' Their prices tended to be higher than what we asked for. But that's happened to us before—I think they do it to get your business. They put too high a price on your house. You lose time, because your house sits on the market a couple of months, then you come down to a more realistic figure."

So you were thinking of using a discount broker?

"I had looked into discount brokers. Instead of charging 6 percent, the man we talked to sets 1-1/2 percent. He does all of the paperwork and handles the phone calls. We contacted him and explored the idea. But we didn't use him. We had time to show the house ourselves. I know, that's not practical for everyone. Not everyone can be at home showing the house, answering phone calls, and setting up appointments."

What about getting a lawyer?

"We had a personal lawyer, and as soon as we sold the house, we contacted him. We advised the buyers to get a lawyer, too."

Did you advertise?

"Yes, but that's not how we sold the house. We sold it through word of mouth—by telling friends and neighbors that we were selling. The ad ran twice before we could tell the paper to take it out. We did pay the discount broker to include an ad, and a photo of our house, in his newsletter.

"I wrote the ad after just reading other ads. I picked out words I liked, the ones describing the nicest features of the house. 'Colonial brick.' 'Center hall.' 'Slate roof.' 'Family room in basement.' 'Fireplace.' 'Brick patio.'

"We got an awful lot of calls from brokers."

Did you spruce up the house?

"The house was in good condition. We had painted the trim the year before, so it looked nice on the outside. The yard was neat and well mowed, with very nice gardens. And we had painted the living room recently. A lot of little things, which don't cost much, can really make a house attractive.

"Actually, a lot needed to be done, and you don't notice until you decide to sell "

Did you do anything to ensure your safety?
"If I didn't have a good feeling about someone who phoned, I'd show it to him only when my husband was home."

How did you show the house?
"Well, I kept all the lights on—I didn't want to lead people through the house in the dark. I had made sure everything was neat, not cluttered. And I pointed out features people might not notice—the storm windows, the electric garage-door opener, the solid brass fixtures, the special woodwork. We told people how much it cost to heat the house. Some seemed to care, some didn't.

"It was strange. I asked myself, 'Is this real? Will I ever hear from these people again?'"

How did you qualify the buyer?
"As it turned out, the people were unusual. They paid cash. There wasn't any mortgage to be approved."

How did the buyers hear about your house?
"A friend of ours was playing tennis with someone, and mentioned that he knew of a house for sale—ours. The other tennis player was interested, and he and his wife came right over.

"Selling our house ourselves was an easy and wonderful thing."

By owner in Sandy, 1,900 sq. ft. 3 bdrms, 2 baths. Fireplace and woodburning stove in fin. basement. Fully landscaped and fenced. 1/2 acre horse property. Many extras! $87,500. Call 745-2090 to see!

185

Linda Larson and her husband, Larry, who live in Utah, are both 35, and when I spoke with her, they had just put their house on the market.

Why are you selling your house by yourself?
"I don't want to pay a real-estate broker's fee. And five years ago, we also sold our house without a broker and got the price we were asking for. It took only two months then. We should have gotten a few thousand more, but we wanted to sell it fast."

How did you set the price—$87,500?
"I just asked neighbors what they were selling their houses for. With the other house we sold, we got an appraisal, which cost $75."

Are there any drawbacks to selling a house yourself?
"If you have the time, there aren't any drawbacks. You just have to be sure to be home to show the house. We did have to do a little painting, and we replaced the carpeting, but we'd have had to do that with or without a broker."

Are buyers dubious about dealing with do-it-yourselfers?
"No, they feel you'll drop the price a little bit since you're not going through an agent."

How long have you been trying to sell your house?
"We just started. We waited until the hunting season was over. Everyone goes deer hunting—no one stays in town. Nothing interrupts them from doing that. And we had to do some painting, so the house wasn't ready."

How do you plan to spread the word your house is for sale?
"We'll have an open house, and put signs in front of

our home and at the end of the street. We've also told our neighbors that we're selling. And we'll run other ads. To write that ad, we read other ads—and thought about what would have attracted us if we were looking for a house. We tried to bring out the best points."

How will you qualify a buyer?
"We have a lawyer at the company where my husband works. We've told him that we're selling, and as soon as we get someone really interested, the lawyer can qualify him."

Are you doing anything to ensure your safety?
"I'm not worried—even if someone drops in unexpectedly because of the sign in front.

"We have three Dobermans, and they always walk at my side."

Charles and Debbie Neumayer of Glen View, Illinois, sold their house without a broker two weeks after putting it on the market. Charles, 29, owns a gas station. The interview was conducted with Debbie, 26.

Were there any drawbacks?
"None at all. I wasn't bored sitting around waiting for the phone to ring, or for buyers to arrive. I just read the newspaper. But we knew that our area sold itself. Our neighbor had also sold his house without a broker. And we did it just to save the 6 percent commission.

"We almost got discouraged, though. Our neighbors had sold their house, and when they ran their ad, the first day they got ten phone calls. The first day my ad ran, I got no calls at all! Then the phone started ringing. We had 18 people over on Saturday, 8 the next day.

"You should set a time limit, though. You might give yourself a month to sell your house yourself."

How did you establish a price?

"We had four brokers give us market evaluations— everyone wants to give you a free market evaluation. The low estimate was $115,000, the high $129,000. We decided we wanted $120,000, so we set the price at $124,500. But we sold for $120,000."

Did you do anything special to spruce up your house?

"We did the stuff we were planning to do to the house all along, but never got around to. It was like straightening up for company. We touched up, spackled, took a lot of the kids' toys out, painted a little, made the closets not look so packed."

Who showed the house, you or your husband?

"My husband was going to do it. Then he decided that he'd rather not. He got rather insulted by people who came by and said, 'Why is the roof angled like this?' "

Did you do anything to ensure your safety?

"I didn't worry about that. I always had a couple of people looking at the same time, and I always had the door open.

"I also put little things away—there was nothing of value around."

When did you hire a lawyer?

"We didn't need legal assistance until the person buying the house gave us a contract."

What about ads in the papers?

"We put ads in the two big Chicago papers and in the local paper. First the *Tribune*, then the *Sun-Times*. People look mostly on Sunday, so that's when most of our ads appeared. We wrote the ad after looking at other ads. The ad told about our open houses. But I think it was the signs we put up at busy intersections that sold the house."

Were there any problems at all?
"Well, people feel funny dealing with the owners. They can't say, 'We don't like the decorating,' or 'We want you to take a couple of thousand off the price.'"

How did you qualify the buyer?
"We really didn't. We don't know how to do it. But the woman who bought our house was an older woman, and she already owned a house. We knew she could afford it."

What advice would you give other homeowners who are thinking of selling their houses themselves?
"Don't get discouraged. In two weeks, I saved $7,000. Thanks heavens I didn't get discouraged!"

Huntington Village
Well kept 3-2-2. New tile, floor drapes. Many extras.
$66,900. By owner. 876-0980

Steve Livington is pessimistic about selling his home without a broker; or, for that matter, *with* a broker. He lives in Houston, where real estate is currently deep down in the basement. His advertisement in the *Houston Post* is surrounded by ads from brokers offering to sell homes foreclosed because their owners couldn't keep up the payments.

Other ads say, "Must sell," "Bargain," "Owner will finance," "A steal," "Assume VA—no money down," and "Free Mercedes if you buy my house in Quail Valley."

Why are you trying to sell your house without a broker?

"We were mainly trying to find out if there was any interest. We need a bigger house. We're in a three-bedroom house, and we'd like a four-bedroom house. And the market in Houston is such that it's great to buy a new or existing house. I don't want to rent this one out, so I thought, 'Let me just find out where the interest is.'

"Maybe the other reason is that I know some other people .in town that have been using a broker without any luck. So I said I'll give myself a month to see if there's any interest at all."

How long have you had your house on the market?

"Three weeks. I've had only two phone calls. Unfortunately, in the Houston area there are so many foreclosures around, that's what people are going for. And you really can't blame them.

"We haven't had any interest, so now we're really thinking, 'Let's stay where we are.' We might expand the house. Because we like it—it's just not big enough. My wife is pregnant with our third child, so three bedrooms is a little . . . cozy."

Have you ever sold a house by yourself before?

"No, but I bought this from the owner, and I found it relatively easy."

Any advice to others who want to sell by themselves?

"Make it look nicer than it's ever been. I put new Italian tile in the entryway, the kitchen, and the dining room. We're also going to put a carpet in the family room.

"The trick is, you've just got to get the right person to walk through the door.

"There's just so much against us in the Houston market now, with the foreclosures, with the reasonable interest rates on new houses. It's a great market for a first-time buyer or someone being transferred in. It's tough for us who live here."

Dennis Rozzelli is a life-insurance agent in his early twenties, selling a house in the Chicago area (Glen Cove) for $220,000.

Why are you selling it yourself?

"We've bought another house for approximately the same amount. We just want to save an extra $12,000, what the broker would charge. So our reason is just financial.

"In this area, selling your house yourself isn't very common. But I prefer it. It's your house, you know a lot about it. Besides, I sell life insurance, so I have experience selling. Though it's not necessarily an asset— houses are different from life insurance."

How did you decide on the offering price?

"We haven't owned the house long, so we're adding the cost of our improvements, like putting a deck in the back. And a little extra. When we purchased the house, it had been on the market for a year and a half. No one had shown any interest. There was no furniture inside—it was vacant. It's easier to imagine living in a house if there's furniture inside. And the house is now quite well decorated. So we expect a good profit."

Do you have a lawyer?
"As soon as we have an agreement with a buyer, we plan to consult a lawyer."

Have you advertised the house?
"We've advertised in all the Chicago-area papers. We mention the open houses we're having. The contents are just the same—the headline says, 'Come Fall in Love.' The ads don't cost much—maybe $20, and that's $140 a week."

How do you go about showing people the house?
"We make everything sound attractive. We explain certain features while we're showing people around, tell them the measurements. We keep the lights on, too, and the curtains open. The house is in mint condition.

"I think it's always very advisable to have a guide pointing out a house's strong points. Some buyers feel uncomfortable, but 85 percent appreciate having a guide."

What about safety precautions?
"I make sure that my wife isn't home alone. And we watch people who come—we're always following them around."

Do you have a fact sheet, describing your house?
"Yes, with a photo of the house, too."

Do you have advice for other do-it-yourselfers?
"Keep at it. Always have your house being shown."

RIDGEWOOD—by owner, newly renovated home in prestigious Salem Ridge area on oversz lot. 3 BRs, 2 bths, LR, enormous DR w/sliding gls drs that open to deck & ingrnd pool, new gourmet kit w/ceramic tile flr, micro, DW, sunny Fla rm, lndry rm, 2 car gar. All new Andersen wndws & new crptng thruout. Many extras. $359,900. 763-8712 aft 6 wkdays, wkends all day.

When I called, this New Jersey man said, "Are you sure you're not a broker?"

On Setting the Price
"The first thing to do is get in as many brokers as possible—10 or 15 of them. Tell them you want a 'market appraisal.' You'll get 10 or 15 different prices—along with 100 arguments why you should use a broker.

"The difference in prices can be up to $100,000. But five or six will be pretty close together, and that price is a ballpark figure. Take the average.

"Brokers warn you not to overprice your house. They really want their 6 percent commission—fast. 'We want to price your house right.' Sure they do. All they want to do is move your house. If you have a $350,000 house, they'll want to move it at $300,000 because it's faster cash for them. They don't want to spend $150 a week for ads. If they can get you to underprice your house—offer a $350,000 house for $300,000—they can sell it in three weeks.

"We let people know it's principals only. If you're saving a 6 percent commission on a $300,000 house, you've got quite a range of money to play with. So we let buyers know we can talk a bit about price. We kind of let people know we're flexible.

"Some people come into our house with a broker, but we won't budge. We're not going to pay $20,000 to a broker.

"One Realtor gave us a low figure. To justify it, she pulled out her listings and found a house like ours that had sold for much less. But we saw that that house had been sold a year and a half ago, and the market was tight then. And she wasn't very smart. Otherwise, she'd have figured that we knew where the house was, and we knew that it sold the first day because it was underpriced. We'd rather put the price high. We can always come down."

On Brokers

"Another house, we sold through a broker, and that soured us on brokers. He was aggressive. 'No, the house is worth only so much,' he told us. We showed him 'comparatives'—similar houses that had been sold—and told him that ours was the nicest house on the block, but he didn't pay attention. It was push push push. So we signed.

"The broker called his wife, she drove someone over, and he bought the house. It sold in 45 minutes because it was underpriced. So you've got to be careful.

"But you can learn a lot from brokers, like the ones we asked for a market appraisal. They can show you which papers they run advertisements in, and tell you the best days. And they can show you comparatives.

"The biggest advantage that brokers have is the multiple-listing service. They can get other brokers from all over the county working to sell our house."

On Fees

"They're all willing to strike a deal, but no one wants to come down from 6 percent. Most said 6, one guy said 5, and one said 4. But the one for 4 couldn't tap a market. You could tell. He didn't have any buyers."

On Ads

"We run ads for about a week, then yank them out. We don't want them to get stale. But we don't run the same ad—we change it around. Maybe we'll adjust the price, then throw it in again.

"If someone sees your house just sitting there at the same price, they'll figure it's a dog.

"Talking about dogs, I saw another ad that said, 'No brokers. MY DOG BITES.'"

On Buyers

"Everything's pretty much what you expect. A lot of people come in here, and you can tell pretty much which are just looking around, joyriding.

"When people come in, you can't take anything they say personally. It's your house and your style of decoration. Some people will come in and won't like something, and will say so. You've got to learn to ignore it."

On Lawyers

"Getting an attorney is the most important thing. He'll tell you, for example, that you want a 10 percent deposit, and you should give the buyer just three business days to get his money back. An attorney can keep on top of things. He can find out where the buyer is getting his financing. He can call up the mortgage company the buyer mentions."

On Qualifying Buyers

"Ask them point blank: Where do you work, what type of income do you have? In this price range, they know their finances. You can also use a rule of thumb. They need double their salaries for any mortgage they want.

"If they tell you they have loans on three cars, are keeping up two other houses, and have no other equity, you know it's going to be tough.

"But you don't have to help them find a mortgage. There are so many mortgage brokers around, these guys can latch on to somebody."

Advice: "The name of the game is to be patient."

EASTLAKE/CENTURY
HILLS Contemporary starter home, skylights, fireplace, heat pump, central air, great room with loft. Cul-de-sac. 2 years old. $46,000. 856-3427, nights and weekends.

A good ad? It should be. The author, Dan Cowan of Lexington, Kentucky, works in the advertising department of a local newspaper.

Cowan reports that readership studies show that home buyers want to know:

- ☑ price
- ☑ location
- ☑ number of square feet
- ☑ number of bedrooms
- ☑ possible financing

Still, he warns, don't include anything negative if you

can avoid it, such as the location if your house is in a somewhat seedy section of town.

After the basics, add whatever special attractions your house has—a fireplace, skylights, central air. (A "great room," mentioned in his ad, is a combination dining room and living room. A "cul-de-sac," of course, is what we old-timers call a dead-end street.)

Cowan can't abide ads that are put together by frustrated writers, the kind that suggest that people can "nestle up close to their fireplace. I believe in being straightforward."

Also, be specific. A feature of a house that discourages one buyer may encourage another. Some people loathe basements (including me—to my mind, their main purpose is to collect water); others like them, for storage. Some people prefer a garage attached to a house, so they can bring the groceries right into the warmth of the kitchen on a wintry day; others don't want gasoline fumes from a car wafting into their living quarters.

By being specific, Cowan says, you'll filter through the buyers who would be interested and filter out the buyers who'd take one look and hurry away—which wouldn't do a whole lot for your confidence in becoming a successful fizzbo.

"If you don't mention something," Cowan adds, "some classified-ad readers may figure the worst." If you don't specify the number of bedrooms, for example, readers will decide that you have only two, especially if you call your house a "starter" home (Cowan, in his ad, calls his home a "starter" because this lets people know that he's selling a smaller, two-bedroom house, which would appeal to couples looking for their first home).

(To refresh your memory on writing ads, turn back to Chapter 8.)

For two months Bruce Leeb and Rona Eagle, young professionals, tried to sell their house in Paramus, New Jersey, without a broker. They then gave up, went with a broker, and sold their house shortly thereafter.

On Their Reasons for Turning to a Broker

"The market just died," says Rona. "We offered our house at the end of May, and signed with a broker after the Fourth of July.

"We didn't know the importance of the seasons. We thought summer would be great to sell a house, but it's poor. People want to *move* during the summer, after buying earlier in the year. Houses that went on the market at the same time ours did, even with brokers, are still unsold.

"We had already bought another house before putting ours up for sale. We wound up selling our house for less than we wanted because we couldn't afford to carry two houses, paying two mortgages, two insurance coverages, running back and forth. What we *should* have done was test the waters—we should have put our house up for sale, and not taken the first offer. But we would have gotten a good idea of how quickly our house would sell, along with the names of prospective buyers. Buying another house without knowing how quickly we could sell ours was a mistake. Even brokers told us that.

"We got a lot of calls at first, then they dwindled. We're very lucky we sold at all.

"We got one offer while we were selling the house ourselves. We had priced the house at $259,900. A buyer, who said he wanted the house for his brother-in-law, offered us $225,000. It came during the second week. He gave us all kinds of excuses why he couldn't offer more. We finally sold the house for $245,000, and paid the broker $14,700. We wound up with $230,000. Maybe we should have accepted the $225,000 offer."

On Price

"We asked some brokers for a market analysis, and we asked our neighbors who had just bought their houses, or who were also selling. Houses in the area were all similar, though ours had an extra family room and an extra bathroom. That's how we decided on $259,900."

On Ads

"We didn't budget an amount for ads. We thought we'd advertise until we sold the house. We wound up spending $450 to $500. We ran ads at least once a week, and sometimes every day. We used different newspapers, too, from the New York Times to the local weekly.

"We found that ads don't have to be lengthy if you describe the key features. When we cut down the size of the ads to save money, there was no difference in the number of phone calls.

"The first question everyone seemed to ask was: 'What's the size of the property?'

"We tried slanting the ads to different audiences. We said it was a mother-and-daughter house, and got calls from just mothers and daughters. Then we said it was a house for a professional, and that didn't sell. Finally we just described the rooms.

"The people who bought the house wanted it as an investment. We never even thought of advertising it to investors."

On Buyers

"First, we packed up all the good things and took our jewelry to the bank.

"We had open houses every weekend. We'd have two groups. I'd take one, then Bruce would take the other—maybe he would show them the outside while the others were waiting. You can't have them wandering around. They need someone to point things out to them.

"We also made appointments during the week. We were as flexible as possible.

"If anyone was interested, they'd spend 40 minutes looking at the house. If they were just looking at our decorations, they'd spend 10 minutes.

"We did have one man who was interested. He came back three or four times, with a plumber or an electrician. He was planning on redesigning the house. But then he found another house, and bought that. So it was close."

On Brokers

"Brokers were always calling. We asked whether they'd take a 3 percent commission instead of 6 if they brought a customer in. The smaller, local brokers said yes, but not the big national firms. But we wound up with a 6 percent broker because we had a lot of confidence in him. He put a price of $270,000 on the house, so that if it sold for that amount we'd clear $253,800—almost what we'd been asking, $259,000. But as I said, we sold for only $245,000.

"The biggest advantage of brokers is that they have access to the multiple-listing service. Our house was sold because another broker—not the one we hired—found a man looking for houses as an investment.'

On Lawyers

"Our lawyer told us to get all offers in writing, and there'd be no deal unless we had 10 percent of the price in our hands. They had to give us an offer in writing, and give us 10 percent of the price within 10 days, before we would stop showing the house.

"We had a standard contract ready, the kind you can get from any stationery store."

On Negotiating

"Our broker and the buyer's broker sat around bargaining. The buyer gave us a contract for $230,000. We rejected it, but counteroffered $260,000. He went up to $240,000, we went down to $250,000. We compromised on $245,000."

SAN MARIN VALLEY, 3 BR, 2-1/2 ba 1560 sq. ft. New carpets, upgrades, spacious living room w/ frplc., formal din. area, eat-in kitchen. Lrg. master suite. Garage. $127,000. Principals only. 897-9280

Diane Thompson is selling her house in California for $127,000 without an agent—and $132,900 if an agent finds a buyer (from which she will realize $124,926 after paying a 6 percent commission). In effect, if she finds a buyer herself, she'll give the buyer two-thirds of the commission fee she would save, but still come out $2,000 ahead.

Why did you decide to sell your house without an agent?

"Our broker even suggested it. We are in a townhouse, and the market right now is very slow for condos and townhouses. A number of people here in the project that

I know had their property listed for months and months without a sale, and then sold their houses by themselves.

"The main reason is to drop that commission off the price and list the house for $6,000 less. That makes it more attractive to a wider market of people. But also, a lot of people, I've found, don't want the pressure, they don't want somebody calling them up every day, 'Well, what are you going to do about this, what are you going to do about that?' They just want to be on their own to make decisions.

"We've already found a house that we want, and the people have been real nice, even trying to help us by sending our For Sale by Owner fliers to their friends."

How did you decide on a selling price?

"Based on sold and closed escrow prices in this project. In California, closings are handled by 'escrow' agents. ['Escrow' refers to handing money, deeds, or other valuables over to a third party—the escrow agent—to keep until the terms of a contract are fulfilled.] Our price is actually a bit lower. There're a number of them on the market now, and they range from 129 to 137, with an agent. For a while we had ours listed at 134 with an agent, then we dropped it to 132.9. That's how we decided to try selling it ourselves for 127."

You mentioned that you had a flier?

"Yes, we have a computer that does graphics. We described the house on the front, and on the back we drew a floor plan. We give it to people so that they'll remember this house. People see so many houses, they can't remember which they've seen. We have every bit of information we think somebody could possibly use. The floor plan has all the closets, the toilet, the tub and

202

everything." (See pages 204–205.)

Are you willing to give a buyer a first or second mortgage?
"We can't. We need the cash for the house we want to buy. If we didn't, it would be a different story."

Did you ever sell a house without a broker?
"We almost did. With the condo before this, we had an exclusive agency listing, which gave us the right to sell it ourselves. We had a Sunday open house, and we had three people who wanted to buy it directly from us. The open house was from 12 to 5, and before it was even over, at 4:30, the agent came in with an offer. That was really fantastic. That night we had the three people call, and they were just furious that the condo had been sold!"

Have you done anything to ensure your safety?
"That's an excellent question. Real-estate agents are being told by their county boards not to sit open houses alone anymore. Four women agents in Seattle were raped during open houses recently. So, yes, my husband is here when the property is shown, and frequently one of us is here when the agent shows the house. But if that's the case, we try to make ourselves scarce because people like to have some freedom in looking around— they don't like being tailgated.

"There are other things you can do. We secured our coin collections out of sight, and I put my good jewelry in the bottom of my lingerie drawer.

"But the important thing is, if somebody wants to come to your house, make sure there's someone with you, even if you have to ask a neighbor. There are a lot of nuts hanging around."

The residence of Charles & Diane Thompson
21 Lotus Court
Novato, CA

Beautifully Decorated
San Marin Valley Townhome
With New Carpet, Wallpaper & Upgrades
3 Bedrooms, 2 and 1/2 Baths

Large Living Room with Fireplace
Formal Dining Area
Large Master Suite with Cathedral Ceilings

Spacious Eat-In Kitchen Including:
Tile Counters, Ample Oak Cabinets, Pantry,
Double Ovens, Dishwasher, Garbage Disposal

Nicely Landscaped Patio
Garage with Electric Door Opener

Professionally Managed, Well Funded Complex
In A Park Like Environment
Pool and Tennis Court
Assumable Loan

$127,000
by Owner

For further information call the Thompson's at (415) 897-9280

204

The Rosewood Model

**3 Bedrooms
2.5 Baths
1560 Square Feet**

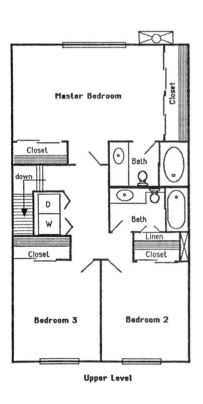

Upper Level

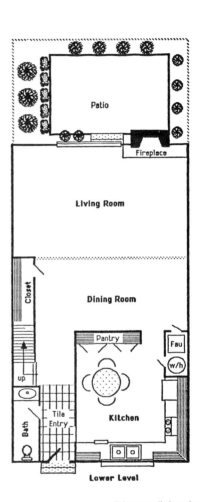

Lower Level

Not necessarily to scale

How would you qualify a buyer?

"Buyers are sometimes a little bit timid and don't want to give information. But if they're genuinely interested in making a sale, they'll tell you where they work, their work history, their salary range.

"If a buyer is going to buy my house, he should go to a lender and get pre-qualified. Some banks even give people letters. That releases me from the headache of worrying whether a buyer's lying, and from running and getting credit reports, and all that. There are many loan brokers that do it, and it's free.

"We ourselves were pre-qualified when we went looking for a house. We thought we could afford a $170,000 house; we were told we could afford a $220,000 house.

"I would never put anything on paper unless a buyer were pre-qualified. For all I know, he has a terrible credit history ten miles long."

Home sellers on the West Coast don't use lawyers, do they?

"Generally, no. Agents out here don't want lawyers getting involved. And if a deal is clear and smooth, you don't need them. The title insurance companies do an awful lot."

How have you gone about spreading the word that your townhouse is for sale?

"Besides sending the flier to everyone I know, I wrote a personal letter, and made enough copies to send everyone three copies.

"The open houses seem to be the thing that gets people in. Buyers don't seem to pay much attention to your ad in the back of the newspaper, but they read the section on open houses.

"We advertised open houses every week, for Sundays from 1 to 5. We serve refreshments only when real-estate agents come—so they will study our house and bring buyers. And, since we secured everything of value, we let people wander upstairs on the second floor by themselves. People stay a little longer if they don't feel you're breathing down their backs."

THREE MONTHS LATER: Have you sold your house yet?

"We sold and closed in escrow. Now we're renting—until the people in the house we bought can move out. This house is in the same area, but it's not the one we'd been thinking about. We looked at 189 houses in six months, so we're sure it's right for us."

Who brought in the buyer, you or an agent?

"We did. He was someone who had seen the house before, and was waiting until he had sold his own house before bidding for ours. His buyer was obtaining a Veterans Administration mortgage, so it took four months. Now we don't owe anyone a commission.

"We sold at $126,000, a thousand dollars less than we wanted. And the buyer got us to share the cost of a termite inspection—$40.

"The buyer signed a standard purchase agreement—there's a store here that specializes in real-estate forms. He paid us only $1,000 as a binder—normally, it's 10 percent—but we were going to escrow in just four weeks, and we knew he was eager to buy the house.

"We saved only a thousand dollars by selling the townhouse ourselves. But if we had tried to sell it for $132,900 instead of $127,000, we might not have sold it at all!"

4 BEDROOMS, 2 BATHS
View, privacy, new deck. Principals only. $255,000.
763-6784

Rich Demarchi of Mill Valley, California, just turned his house over to a broker, despairing of trying to sell it himself.

Why?
"I got calls, I had people. look at it, but I didn't get enough. It was just a matter of having to expose it to a lot of people, that's all.

"See, it's not just a regular piece of property. It has individual things that you either hate or love. It's that sort of situation. So, on that basis, it's harder to sell than a tract home. It's on a hillside, there are stairs to the house, things like that. So I listed it."

What price are you asking now?
"I got them to list it for a 5 percent commission, not 6 percent, and I had to raise my price from 255 to 260 to cover part of the commission.

"The whole theory of real estate is that sellers don't want to pay the commission. Well, they just make the buyers pay more, to cover the commission—that's all it is.

"The buyer would be better off buying from me, because he would save. I could have sold it to him for 245 and come out just where I wanted to, but now with a broker I have to sell it at a minimum of 255 to come out where I want to. Brokers like to tell you it doesn't work out that way, but it does."

Were you willing to help a buyer with the financing?
"No, no. I need the cash to put into another property."

Did you do anything special to ensure your safety?
"No, that doesn't bother me."

How did you plan to qualify a buyer?
"I'd sit down with them right here, and I'd ask them how much he wants to put down, roughly, and how much he makes, and I'd put those two figures together. Then I'd call a couple of lending institutions and give them the figures, and if they say it's in the ballpark, okay. If not, I'd just call them back and say, 'Hey, you can't qualify, no sense going ahead.' The two major things are income and the percentage you want to put down."

In retrospect, would you have done things differently?
"I've sold property by myself before, but commercial property. It was kind of a chancy thing to try it by myself because it's a hard-to-find location. My mother has a house in West Lake, and that would have been a different story. It's a tract area, and houses sell pretty quickly because a lot of people go by the area. Nobody can see my house. I tried to sell it myself, just to give it a shot, but the statistics are against you when you have isolated property."

MAGNOLIA
Open 2-5 pm
2916 E. Flynn. $129,000
View of Sound. 3 BR, 2 full BA. Lrg. deck overlooking beautiful priv. bkyard. Full bsmt. part finished for extra liv. space. Close to Village. By owner.
745-2546

Mr. and Mrs. Bolten of Bothell, Washington, sold their house themselves, four months after having put it on the market. We spoke to Mrs. Bolten.

Why did you decide to sell without a broker?
"My husband and I have been in real-estate transactions before, and we figured we knew quite a bit about it. My husband is retired, so he wouldn't be taking time off from work to do it. We also figured he would do a better job than the broker because the broker's got a lot of other people to look after."

Did you run ads, put up signs, have open houses?
"All three. We ran an ad once a week, usually on a Saturday and Sunday, in one or two papers. And we had an open house every Saturday and every Sunday, which a broker isn't going to do for you. We also had For Sale signs out in front, and signs on the nearby street corners, with House for Sale on them along with arrows."

Any tips about writing newspaper ads?
"One of the most important things is: Put in 'For Sale by Owner.' Many people don't trust brokers. And they think sellers selling by themselves will be easier to deal with."

You must have gotten calls from brokers.
"Oh, my lord."

How did you learn about real estate?
"I took a real-estate course once, and I passed the test and was going to sell real estate. But then I discovered that we were going to have a baby, so I quit. But we always have kept our hand in, mainly because we move around a lot. We usually sell our houses by ourselves."

Any advice for other home sellers?

"Mainly, they should know something about what they're doing. If they know absolutely nothing, they should either get advice or stay out of it. Because there are pitfalls."

GRNWD 3 BR. By owner. Open Sun. 752 N. 56th. $74,950. 453-7809

Clay and Carol Kean tried but failed to sell their house without a broker. They finally sold their house with a broker who charged only a 5 percent commission, not the 7 percent rate that's common in Seattle.

Why did you try selling without a broker, Mrs. Kean?
"Well, my husband felt that we were the ones who put all of the money into it and all the time and effort. He didn't want to pay the broker 7 percent."

How long had you been trying?
"About four weeks."

Had you had any interest?
"We had a lot of people come, and a lot of brokers and agents. The brokers tell us that a house in our price range can't be sold without a broker because you're selling to an unsophisticated market. They don't even know how to make an offer. And I guess I agree.

"We've told people that we've talked to a mortgage company, and they'd be willing to talk to people, but it didn't help. We've had 30 or 40 people look at the house, and not one offer.

"Maybe people are afraid of bargaining with an owner, making a low offer. When my husband bought a home through an agent, my husband's pretty aggressive,

211

and he'd make very low offers. One time, the agent didn't want to present the offer, but he did, and the guy accepted it. And so our agent said, 'If I'd known he would have accepted that, *I'd* have offered it myself and gotten rich.'

"And some people aren't brave like that."

Did you do anything to ensure your safety?

"You know, I didn't, and a few times I was there by myself.

"I asked some real-estate women friends if they carry a gun or something, and they said no. A few times I had a little fear come over me, like what would I do if . . .

"But usually my husband stays here, or we stay together.

"I was with an agent in a $350,000 home once, in a secluded area, and this retarded person came up to the door. He wanted to rent the house for $40 a month. I mean, he was perfectly harmless, but there could be weirdos.

"Still, I don't know how a woman agent is protected."

How were you going to qualify a buyer?

"We were going to have them get their own loan. We wanted the cash out. Because capital-gains taxes are going up, we felt this was a good time to get our money out."

Did you have a fact sheet?

"Yes, we had one typed up, and we've got gobs of copies. We have two different ones—one that says, 'All reasonable offers considered,' to give someone encouragement to make an offer, and another one, where we took that out. This agent told us that it's like saying your price isn't firm and you'll accept anything. We

212

originally priced it at $79,950, and, after checking around, we lowered it to $69,950."

FOR SALE BY OWNER

Single-family residence located at 752 N. 56th; walking distance to shopping and buses, two bedrooms, full bath, living room, kitchen with eating space Oil heat, full basement with one bedroom, utility space, separate entry.

Features

* leaded windows
* closet windows main floor
* hardwood floors
* fenced backyard
* fireplace
* garage

* lot size 30x100 ft.
* fruit trees
* sidewalks
* 2 miles Greenlake
* shopping Northgate/ Greenwood 5 min.

ASKING PRICE $74,950.00

All reasonable offers considered. Contact Clay or Carole Kean
Phone 453-7809.

ELMWOOD PARK—2 fam, 2BR ea apt., asking $179,900 Owner has NJRE license. 845-0816

Patric Barklow is 31, tall, red-haired and red-bearded, open and frank. He buys and sells houses part time. Full time, he works for a company that makes ballet slippers. The house he's selling is one he's living in; he plans to move into another he's having built.

On Mistakes Sellers Make

"Most people I have met who are selling their own homes don't do it correctly.

"They don't screen people to get enough information to qualify them. They're too willing to accept binders without qualifying people. To qualify them, you've got to ask questions. Find out their place of employment; certify their deposits in a bank. You could get a credit check, but it might cost you $150.

"A lot of people also wait too long before putting their houses on the market. Then they buy a house before selling theirs, and wind up carrying two houses—which costs money. Give yourself a lot of time to sell your house.

"And owners don't get the word around the neighborhood that they're selling their houses. Your best prospects are the friends or relatives of a neighbor. Who knows the area better than your neighbors? They can give buyers as much information as you can, and if a buyer's friends or relatives say it, he'll believe it. Yet I've heard sellers say, 'I don't want to tell my neighbors.' Often it's the best source of leads. I send notes to neighbors within a two- to three-block radius telling them I have a house for sale. Spreading the word through a church or synagogue is also a good idea.

"Most sellers have no idea about contracts. These days, salespeople don't accept binders—they go directly into short contracts, which carry more weight. After signing the contract, the buyer has 3 days to review it, then 10 to 14 days to meet with the attorneys. The binder used to be $100, but now it's $1,000. When the buyer meets with the attorneys, it's 10 percent of the purchase price. I keep contracts in my house, and not many other sellers do.

"Basically, sellers don't have a *plan*. They don't set the right price, they don't spread the word, they don't qualify people, they don't have contracts in their house."

On Price

"I set my price at a little more than similar houses have recently sold for, but a little less than similar houses on the market now. The right price, more than anything, sells a house. When people sell houses on their own, they tend to overprice them. Most owners, when you offer them a lower price than they're asking, get excited and insulted. But you can't let your emotions get in the way. If a buyer offers less than I want, I just say, 'I'll consider it'—and continue trying to sell it on my own.

"To set the right price on your house, you need a good feel for the market. You've got to study what's being advertised, and even look at a few similar houses. Too often, people hear that a neighbor sold a house for $150,000, and that's their entire guide to the price they set on their own house. They don't know whether their neighbor's house was overpriced or underpriced. So, don't go by just one house that's sold recently.

"You *can* overprice your house a little. In today's market, if you wait a while, the market will catch up to your price. Besides, it's hard to *raise* your price once you've set it, but you can always come down.

"I bought the house I'm selling from a woman who was selling it herself, and she had a real-estate license, too. She was selling it for less than it was worth—a couple of thousand dollars less. A few people made full-price offers. When she told them she had offers, they went up, bidding more than the asking price. I told her I'd beat all offers she got, and that's how I landed the house."

On Ads

"I run one ad and see how it draws. I choose the best paper—the one with the most real-estate ads. Here in

New Jersey, it's *The Record*. It has a discount for Wednesdays and Sundays, and that's enough. I skip the following week. I see how many people called, how many showed up. I might change the price if there wasn't enough interest.

"If you priced the house correctly, there's no need to give much information in the ad—people should phone. You don't want to tell *everything*. You just want to give enough so people will call. That's what an ad is for, to generate calls. Just mention the points in the house—the number of bedrooms, the fireplace, whatever."

On How Long to Give Yourself

"I won't give up trying to sell my house myself, because I'm a broker. I belong to three multiple-listing services, and I can use them if I have to. I've set a fair price, so I'm confident."

On Safety

"If I were worried, I would try to qualify people over the phone, before they came. I'd ask for their names and place of employment, and call to check. I wouldn't make an appointment until I'd checked them out. Otherwise, to protect yourself, you can get help. Have other people over when you show your house."

On Open Houses

"I don't let people enter without signing a sheet with their name and address, so I can call them back if they seem interested. And I don't let anyone wander around without me. If two people come at once, I have one wait. I serve coffee and lemonade.

"But there should never be just one person running an

open house. You need one person to greet people, one to show people around."

On Brokers

"Use brokers to your advantage. If one says, 'We have people who are interested,' tell him they're welcome to come by. If he says, 'You have to sign up,' say no. If he's confident, he'll bring people by. Tell him that since he won't have to split a fee with any other agent, you'll pay him a 3 percent commission if he finds you a buyer at your asking price. Sign a statement to that effect. And ask him to put the names of the buyers he has on the statement.

"If I ever signed with a broker, I'd give him three months to sell my house. I'd make sure he was a member of the multiple-listing service, and get a guarantee that he'd advertise my house once a week. At *least*."

On Helping Buyers Financially

"It depends on your situation. But if you want to help with the financing, get professional help. You must know what you're doing. Don't jump in. It's *very* hard to foreclose."

On Lawyers

"I don't trust lawyers. I've been lied to and dragged around. To find a good lawyer, ask someone who's used one and was satisfied. A good reference is worth more than anything else."

On the Closing

"I don't use the word 'contract.' It scares people. I say 'purchase agreement.' I say 'endorsement,' not 'signature.' I tell a buyer, 'Why don't you endorse this, so we can get started on the rest of the work?' "

Arthur M. Watkins of Piermont, New York, sold his house without a broker—of course. He's an engineer, and the author of a slew of books on housing, including *How to Avoid the Ten Biggest Home-Buying Traps.*

What are the advantages of selling without a broker?
"Heck, saving the commission. You can save thousands of dollars. The biggest disadvantage is that a lot of sellers can't dicker. They don't know about adding 5 or 10 percent to the price, then coming down during the give and take."

What mistakes do sellers make?
"Overpricing may be the biggest one. Particularly these days, when the market's been leveling off. A lot of people have inflated ideas about their houses' value; they're blinded by the opportunity to make a small fortune.

"If you overprice your house and it doesn't sell for a while, people may get suspicious. And if they know it's been on the market for a while, they're likely to offer you less money. And you may have to come down—and you never know *how far* down.

"Brokers can give you an idea about prices, but they tend to tell sellers that their houses are worth more than they are, just to get an exclusive listing."

How did you set a price on your own house?
"I did it the right way. I hired an appraiser. He had no vested interest in overpricing the house (I'm using the asexual 'he'). Three out of four sellers won't spend the

218

dough on an appraiser. They want cheap advice and they get cheap advice. Call a bank or mortgage broker for names of appraisers, or look them up in the phone book. Find someone with a professional certification. These appraisers know the history of house prices in your area, and know what the last two or three have sold for."

Do you have any tips on writing goods ads?

"Here's some advice for all writers: State the facts. Don't lay it on. Remember what Flaubert said—The adjective is the enemy of the noun

"Read the other ads for ideas. And see which papers in your area carry the most real-estate ads."

What about sprucing up your house?

"Remember that first impressions last. Drive up to your house as if you were a buyer, and see what strikes you. Does everything look neat and well-kept? Or is the paint cracked or peeling? Is the handle to the front door tarnished? Don't repaint the exterior unless it's in very bad shape—only have it touched up.

"Don't spend a lot of money on fancy decorations or fancy wallpaper. Almost everyone has different ideas of what colors are best, what pattern of wallpaper. Don't even repaint the inside even if the colors are fading.

"But make sure you fill in cracks or holes—anything that might suggest there's a structural problem.

"And make sure you clean up the cellar. A lot of people don't. And yet that's what many buyers see last—and *last* impressions can last, too."

How should you go about showing your house?

"First of all, screen your buyers. Don't let them come in until you've qualified them. Get their names, addresses, and phone numbers. Ask them where they work. Ask whether they can afford your house, and whether they've made financing arrangements.

"Some burglars pose as buyers when they want to case your house. That's why I never have 'open house.'

"When you show buyers through your house, be low key. Don't oversell. Answer their questions. And make sure you give them a fact sheet, stressing features that aren't visible. Mention in it the heating and electrical bills and the taxes—and be ready to document them. Stick to the facts. And when you walk around with the people, observe them—see what interests them."

How do you coax buyers to make an offer?

"Before they leave, ask them—in a low-key way— whether they're interested. Is there anything else they want to know?"

When should you hire a lawyer?

"You should hook up with a lawyer right away. And you should have a binder or a contract in your house, ready to be signed."

Would you ever help people with the financing?

"Heck, no. But you might check with your bank on what mortgage terms it will give, based on the appraisal you've gotten. And find out whether your mortgage can be assumed. That can cut down on closing costs. And maybe your old interest rate is so low, it will make your house more appealing."

Did you have any trouble selling your own house without a broker?

"I had no problems. I ran an ad in the *Times*, and the first Sunday, ten people came. A celebrity bought it. He was a difficult guy to deal with. I made a mistake in not getting him to give me a deposit and sign a binder. Later,

I went through hell getting him to sign. He was really reluctant to put down any of his money.

"I gave in a little bit on the price. I wanted to give him a nudge, so I went down by a thousand. My wife was mad at me.

"But ours was a very desirable house—an old Victorian with a great view of the river, a good kitchen, and good bathrooms."

TWENTY TIPS ON BUYING A HOUSE

1. CONSIDER HIRING A "BUYER'S BROKER"

A buyer's agent owes you loyalty, not the seller. You pay such an agent by the hour ($75, say), or a flat fee ($1,000 to $5,000), or a percentage of your purchase price (say 3 percent). By dickering with the seller's agent or the seller, your agent may even wrest back the fee you're to pay. By astute bargaining, of course, your agent may also induce a seller to lower the asking price substantially.

There are other benefits of using a buyer's agent:

□ You should procure frank, unbiased information about the better

16

places to live, the better parts of town—where the school system is superior, where house prices have been rising the fastest and steadiest. You should also learn where *not* to live—neighborhoods that are deteriorating, where there are problems with schools, with vandalism, with wet basements.

□ You may have more houses to choose from. Buyer's agents are usually welcomed by fizzbos (you remember *them*), because they will not charge a commission. Even homeowners who aren't thinking of selling may reconsider when they realize that they can save a commission. (Warning to fizzbos: If you're dealing with a buyer's agent, it's two against one. Be wary.)

□ A buyer's agent can negotiate other terms besides the selling price—such as whether the appliances go with the house, the move-in day, and contingency clauses (for example, the deal is off unless you can obtain a mortgage or trust deed on excellent terms).

House hunters unfamiliar with an area in which they are looking may be the most suitable clients for a buyer's agent.

You can invite any agent you respect to become your own agent. But first ascertain how such an agent will deal with the conflict of loyalties in showing you houses she's already got listed. (One solution: The agent obtains your written consent, and the seller's, to represent both of you.)

For a list of 350 agents in 37 states who have had experience and training in representing buyers, you can send $25.00 (plus $2.40 for handling) to Buyer's Broker Registry, P.O. Box 23265, Ventura, CA 93002. Buyer's agents flourish mainly in the West, though; there's only one listed for the entire state of New Jersey.

2. SHOP MOSTLY IN THE SPRING

True, houses may be bargains in other seasons. But you will have more choices during the spring and early summer—and there may be a few bargains then, too. But in a high-priced community (Greenwich, Connecticut; Ridgewood, New Jersey; and so forth) you may be wiser shopping in the winter, when prices will be lower because of low demand, simply so you can afford a house there.

3. KNOW WHAT YOU WANT, AND WHERE

While you should ordinarily examine a great many houses before you buy (say, fifteen at least), don't go overboard. Don't waste time looking at Cape Cods if you definitely want a Colonial, at houses with septic-tank systems if you want a sewage-disposal system, or at houses in Glen Rock if your heart is set on Ridgewood.

The following is a short refresher course on styles of houses:

☐ **Colonials.** Two-story houses. Good for young families, not so good for the elderly. Benefits: Bedrooms

225

and entertainment areas are separate, so you can hold raucous parties while the kids sleep. Heating and cooling costs will be cheaper than in a one-story house. Less costly to build, too, because you don't need a large foundation or large roof. Drawbacks: Lots of stair climbing. In a fire, second-floor rooms are bad places to be.

□ **Split-entries.** The entrance is a foyer; you climb up, or down. Benefits: The basement is fairly high, so it receives more light—and perhaps less water. Drawbacks: Lots of stair climbing. It may be hard to keep the lower level at an even temperature.

□ **Split-levels.** The living area is on entry level; a short flight of steps leads down to the social area, and a short flight leads up to the sleeping quarters. Benefits: Good design for a sloping lot. Flow of interior traffic is smooth. Drawbacks: Lots of stair climbing. Bedrooms may be too warm (heat rises).

☐ **Ranches.** One story. Good for the elderly. Benefits: Hardly any stair climbing. Easy to clean inside, easy to repair outside (you can easily climb onto the roof). Adaptable for life both indoors and outdoors. Drawbacks: Requires a large lot, foundation, and roof, along with long walls. Hence, it is costly to build, and costly to heat and cool. And it's hard to have noisy parties with the kids sleeping on the same floor.

☐ **Cape Cods.** One and a half stories. Benefit: Heating costs are low. Drawbacks: Many owners turn the attic

227

into bedrooms and, without proper attic insulation, the entire house may be too cold in the winter, too warm in the summer. Second-floor rooms may be small, with small windows as well. Not a favorite house style in general.

□ **Tudors** (actually, **Elizabethans**). Two or two and a half stories; the stucco or stone walls have half timbers imbedded in them. Benefits: Striking appearance. Has the advantage of a Colonial. Drawbacks: The unusual roof angles make the house more likely to develop leaks. The house may also be hard to heat and cool evenly. The second-story rooms may be dark because of the roof's peaks and valleys.

Besides choosing a house style or styles that appeal to you, decide whether you want a new house or an existing house.

New houses cost more—and the gap between them and existing houses, which once was about 15 percent, seems to be widening. They have better insulation, newer appliances, better electrical and plumbing systems. Major repairs will be unlikely for years; in any case, you may be given a house warranty. A new house will probably have whatever is fashionable these days, from fireplaces to foyers.

Existing houses are more numerous—by a factor of 50. So you'll have a larger pool to choose from. They're better located—they were there first (closer to schools, for example). They probably were built with better materials and greater care. They have mature trees and shrubbery. Their flaws—from cracked basement walls to dampness in the basement—will be more readily apparent (a plus).

4. BY AND LARGE, USE MORE THAN ONE BROKERAGE FIRM

If an agent truly impresses you, you might throw in with that one person, trusting that he will show you not only houses listed with his agency, but others in the multiple-listing service. You are best advised to choose someone with plenty of experience (not someone who will be selling used cars next year)—for instance, a Realtor (broker) or Associate Realtor (salesperson); someone with advanced degrees, like Graduate of the Realtor Institute and Certified Residential Specialist; and someone who readily confesses, "While I'll try to be fair to you, I'm in the pocket of the homeowners."

The trouble with using just one brokerage firm:

☐ An agent may push houses her firm has listed.

☐ If the agent has shown you a slew of houses, you may feel guilty buying a house for sale by the owner, or a house outside the agent's areas.

Besides, if you use more than one agent, and you are all ready to buy a house that agent Jones has shown you,

229

you can ask agent Smith what he thinks of that house—and learn about its flaws and the neighborhood's flaws.

5. ASK THE SELLER POINTED QUESTIONS

☐ Has the house been tested for radon?

☐ Have there ever been toxic-waste dumps nearby?

☐ Has the house been termite-proofed? If so, what damage had the termites done? Have there been regular termite inspections since then?

☐ Will there be assessments soon for sewers or repaving? For higher taxes?

☐ What are the heating and cooling costs? Are the bills you have shown me recent bills? Could I see older bills, too? (The sellers may have deliberately kept the bills low during the past year.)

☐ Has the heating system ever failed to keep the house warm? Has the cooling system been sufficient to cool the house?

☐ Do fuses blow, or circuit breakers open, often? Can you keep all the air conditioners, or the central air, going at the same time as the toaster, the microwave oven, the vacuum cleaner, and other appliances?

☐ Is the basement perfectly dry? Even after a rainstorm? Why are the nails in the floorboards down there so rusty? Why are there waterstains on the walls? If the basement was ever flooded, what damage was done?

☐ Does the roof leak? Has it ever leaked?

☐ Are there any easements on the property? (A neighbor can legally share the driveway, for instance.) Are there any defects in the title? (The spouse of a former owner may be contesting the sale.)

☐ Is there anything about the house that might lower its value—such as the fact that it's in a flood plain?

Ask your questions in front of the agent. If the seller fibs the agent may spill the beans, knowing that if you ever sue, you will certainly sue the agent, too. (The seller may have taken off for parts unknown. And while courts may consider sellers and buyers amateurs, they tend to throw the book at professional real-estate agents.)

6. REMEMBER THAT AGENTS WORK FOR SELLERS

Never tell an agent that you must move quickly because you have just sold your house, or your apartment lease is up; or that a house you are considering would be perfect for your grand piano or four cars; or that you will offer $87,000, then go up to $92,000 (all of this information may be conveyed to the seller).

7. NEVER BUY A HOUSE WITHOUT HAVING IT CHECKED BY AN INSPECTOR

For a free directory, write to the American Society of Home Inspectors, 1010 Wisconsin Ave., N.W., Suite 630, Washington, D.C. 20007; (202)842-3096. Some states have few or no inspectors (those few are, ideally, engineers). Try builders with good reputations instead. Expect to pay a few hundred dollars.

8. READ BOOKS WRITTEN BY BROKERS FOR OTHER BROKERS

It's an enlightening, appalling experience. One broker counsels his colleagues to be content to sell anyone a house "you personally think is a dog." Another suggests that agents quickly counter *any* objection a buyer

231

makes: "The basement smells moldy"; response: "Room deodorant is cheap." And, of course, there's always the leave-'em-laughing tactic: Show buyers a series of dreadful, dreary shacks, winding up with a fairly decent house, which will look like San Simeon by comparison.

9. HIRE A LAWYER EARLY

The lawyer will not only check documents for you and attend the settlement. She can also give you advice about where to buy and how to negotiate; tell you which brokers have the most listings, which agents are fair and honest with buyers.

10. KEEP A NOTEBOOK ON HOUSES YOU HAVE SEEN

Otherwise, they may blur in your mind. Also, with a notebook, you can warn agent Smith whether agent Jones has already shown you a house. Even record the addresses of houses you drove past because you didn't like their appearance outside.

Next to each house listed, briefly describe its benefits and drawbacks.

Charles and Diane Thompson, whom we met in Chapter 15, stored in their computer the list of houses they had seen. That's how they know they looked at 189. But they didn't record houses they merely drove past, so 189 is low. And they used only one agent to buy their new house. "He deserved his commission," says Mrs. Thompson.

11. DON'T SIGN ANYTHING WITHOUT
    CONTINGENCIES

Such as:

One: "Subject to the approval of my lawyer."

Two: "Subject to a satisfactory report from a house inspector and termite inspector." (Some house inspectors don't do termite inspections.)

Three: "Subject to my obtaining a mortgage for ___ years for ___ at a ___ interest rate." (But remember what I told *sellers* about a clause like this.)

And any others you may think of.

12. FIND OUT HOW LONG A HOUSE HAS BEEN
    ON THE MARKET

Ask the seller or the seller's agent. If a house has been a drag on the market, other buyers may know something you don't know. Or the price may be very high.

13. DON'T BUY THE MOST EXPENSIVE HOUSE IN
    TOWN—OR ON THE BLOCK

You may have trouble selling it later on. Buyers who can afford such expensive houses may shop in better (higher-priced) communities or neighborhoods.

14. BE DUBIOUS OF A HOUSE ON A STEEP HILL

The road may be dangerous in wet weather; you and your children probably won't be able to use a bicycle on it; unless your house is on the crest of the hill, it may have water problems.

15. AVOID A BUSY THOROUGHFARE

You may not have children, but—when you sell—you will find that many prospective buyers do. Besides, pulling your car out of your driveway can be murder.

Also be dubious of a street next to a busy thoroughfare. Drivers may use it to bypass the busier street, making it almost as congested.

16. INSPECT THE AREA WITHIN A HALF-MILE OF A HOUSE

Look for noisy factories, lots of traffic, run-down houses.

17. BE SKEPTICAL OF CORNER LOTS

Removing the snow or leaves from the combined sidewalks may seem like one of the labors of Hercules. And you may not have much privacy in your backyard.

18. BEFORE BUYING A HOUSE, SCREEN IT AGAINST A CHECKLIST

The list on the facing page comes from the U.S. Department of Housing and Urban Development.

19. FIND OUT HOW MUCH HOUSE YOU CAN AFFORD

Sit down with a mortgage lender and fill out an application form. Houses aren't appreciating like mad anymore, so don't regard a house as mainly an investment. Reread Chapter 10.

NEIGHBORHOOD CHECKLIST

Neighborhood Quality

Yes No

1. Are the homes well taken care of? ☐ ☐
2. Are there good public services (police, fire)? ☐ ☐
3. Are there paved roads? ☐ ☐
4. Are there sidewalks? ☐ ☐
5. Is there adequate street lighting? ☐ ☐
6. Is there a city sewer system? ☐ ☐
7. Is there a safe public water supply? ☐ ☐
8. Are the public schools good? ☐ ☐

Neighborhood Convenience

1. Will you be near your work? ☐ ☐
2. Are there schools nearby? ☐ ☐
3. Are there shopping centers nearby? ☐ ☐
4. Is public transportation available? ☐ ☐
5. Will you be near child-care services? ☐ ☐
6. Are hospitals, clinics, or doctors close by? ☐ ☐
7. Is there a park or playground nearby? ☐ ☐

Neighbors

1. Will you be near friends or relatives? ☐ ☐
2. Will you be near other children of your kids' ages? ☐ ☐
3. Will you feel comfortable with the neighbors? ☐ ☐
4. Is there an active community group? ☐ ☐

Does the Neighborhood Have any Problems, Such as:

1. Increasing real-estate taxes? ☐ ☐
2. Decreasing prices of homes? ☐ ☐
3. Lots of families moving away? ☐ ☐
4. Heavy traffic or noise? ☐ ☐
5. Litter or pollution? ☐ ☐
6. Factories or heavy industry? ☐ ☐
7. Businesses closing down? ☐ ☐
8. Vacant houses or buildings? ☐ ☐
9. Increasing crime or vandalism? ☐ ☐

What is your overall rating of the neighborhood?

Good Fair Poor
☐ ☐ ☐

235

20. PAY SPECIAL ATTENTION TO HOUSES BEING SOLD BY THEIR OWNERS

Because the seller is saving on a commission, you may get a good house at an especially good price.

Besides, fizzbos tend to be unusually interesting and decent people.

INDEX